Cilley Family

By

J. P. Cilley

CILLEY FAMILY.

By J. P. Cilley

Some of the family object to the implied derivation of the name in my first article, and refer me to the Scilly Isles, formerly spelled Silly, Silley and Scilley, and whose old British appellation was Syllah, signifying " rock consecrated to the sun."

I am also referred to a rare pamphlet, in the Philadelphia Library, by Francis Gawler, London, 1659. On page 271 of the volume and 21 of the pamphlet, entitled "A Record of some persecutions inflicted upon some of the Servants of the Lord in South Wales," &c.,—meaning Quakers,—appears the following incidental mention of the name: "Again Mary Richard and Mary Moss of Pennarth in *Cilley* for clearing their conscience to John Cutts, Priest were haled, and beaten and drawn up a pair of stairs and their feet in the stocks by the Constable and Priestman."

This is in vicinity of the supposed origin of the family in Somerset Co., Eng., and with the fact, that the families of Cutts and Cilley were contemporary. in N. H., may account for the name. Others insist on the authority of Burke, that the name is of Norman origin, and pursue a zigzag course through the Oxford Chronological tables and the Advent of Saxons into Normandy till they place themselves in Germany and pounce on the town of Cilli,— spelled also Cilly and Cilley,—in the Southern part of Styria, and commence the genealogy thusly:

1   Count of Cilli.
        Children:

2 i   Barbarra[2], Countess of Cilli, m. Sigismund, Emperor of Austria and Hungary.
        Only child:

3 i   Elizabeth[3], m. Albert, who was made Emperor of Austria and Hungary by Sigismond. She died Dec. 24, 1442, and Albert Oct. 17, 1439, from eating melons.
        Children:

4 i   Anne[4], b. — —, m. William, Duke of Saxony.

5 ii Elizabeth[4], b. — —, m. Casimo, King of Poland.

6 iii Ladislaus[4], a posthumos son over whom, in his minority, the Count of Cilli was guardian, and who afterwards succeeded his father on the throne of Austria and Hungary.

  And so down the line to

1001 Simon Cilley,* b. Apr. 1, 1877.

But when we read that the 2 Barbarra,[2] for her libertine conduct, was called the German Messalina, and is described by an Austrian historian as "one who believed neither God, angels or devil—neither hell or heaven," and consider the trouble the family might make in Europe by claiming their rights of succession, we turn with infinite relief to the fisherman magistrate of the Isles of Shoals and make peace in the family by saying that the undoubted origin of the name was from the amphibious occupations of its early members as fishermen and mariners, called Sea-ly (sea-like). It thus appears on the early records of the Isles of Shoals, written in a bold and very legible manner.

When the owners of the name left the sea for the land, the spelling of the name for two or three generations floundered about like a fish out of water, until Gen. Cilley, by his revolutionary fame, anchored it as Cilley.

I have been unable to connect the Isles of Shoals Sealys with Capt. Robert Seely, though it is evident they came from the same part of England. My only authority for making the three brothers of the Isles of Shoals sons of Capt. Robert, is that they might have been drawn East from Watertown, Mass., to the rocky Isles then bustling with enterprise and profit, but only inviting to young unmarried men who could "rough it," while their father was drawn to the more domestic surroundings of Connecticut.

The names Seelye and Seele are found in Massachusetts, while Seeley occurs frequently in Connecticut, New Jersey and Pennsylvania.

1 Capt. Robert Seely, Watertown, Mass., 1630, m. Mary, who had administration of his estate 19 Oct. 1668. Children :

---

* It may be interesting to know that young Simon already exhibits many traits of his early ancestors. He evidently does not believe any more than Barbarra, and is inclined to raise the old boy nights.

2 i ? John (Seely), Isles of Shoals, 1647, appears as commander of the ship Dolphin
by power of attorney given him 11 Sept., 1659, in London (1); owned
property on Star Island which was sold May 3 and June 19, 1651 (2). In
1660 he bought land on the Great Island, near Portsmouth (3). Died
near 1670, while absent at sea; probably not married (4).

† 3 ii ? William (Sealy), probably the same whose deposition, (5) dated June 5, 1670,
represents him as aged about 39. This deposition was sworn to before
John Hunkinge of the Shoals, and speaks of Capt. Fountain, Mr. Green-
land, and his own house, and also the same whose name appears as a
signer to a writing (6) dated Apr. 5, 164(5?).

† 4 iii ? Richard.

5 iv   Nathaniel.

6 v ? Obadiah.

The following I cannot place: George, Isles of Shoals, 1653;
John, Old Norfolk, æ 24 in 1672, and Thomas Sellia, at Saco, 8
Sept., 1665.

3 William[2] (Sealy) m. Elizabeth. The known facts of his life
appear in previous article. Elizabeth, in a deposition dated 27
June, 1674, is represented as about 36 years of age, and may have
been a second wife. Children:

7 i   Emma, m. John Ruel in 1668 or later.

8 ii   Dorcas, m. Jas. Gibbins, Jr., 1668 or later.

4 Richard[2] (Sealy), magistrate Isles of Shoals, 1653. Removed to Hampton Falls. Children:

9 i   Martha, m. John Cluff Jan. 15, 1686.

† 10 ii   Thomas, m. Mary Stanyan before 1697.

† 11 iii   Benoni, m. —— ——.

5 Nathaniel, m. 1st at Fairfield, Conn., 1649, Mary, dau. of
Benj. Turner; 2d late in 1674, Elizabeth, widow of Obediah Gil-
bert, former widow of Nehemiah Olmstead. Killed in action 19
Dec., 1675. Children:

i Nathaniel; ii Robert; iii Benjamin; iv Joseph; v John; vi Mary; vii Sarah;
viii Phebe; ix Rebecca.

6 Obadiah, Stamford, Conn., m. the widow of John Miller of
S., and d. 1657. Children:

i Obadiah; ii Cornelius; iii Jonas.

10 Thomas[3] (Seally), sea captain, Hampton Falls, at Nottingham, at Andover with his son Thomas for a time, and died at his
son Joseph's while on a visit to Nottingham from Andover; m.
Ann Stanyan, dau. of John Stanyan and Mary Bradbury. Children:

12 i   Mary, b. 2 July, 1697; m. Daniel Lovering Dec. 14, 1724.

† 13 ii   John, b. 6 June, 1699; spelled his name Sellea (7); m. Elizabeth E. Glidden (8), dau. of John Glidden of Exeter; remov. to Biddeford (9) 1734-5.

14 iii   Abigail, b. 19 April, 1700.

† 15 iv   Joseph, b. 6 Oct., 1701.

16 v ?   Anne, b, ——; m. Samuel Blake Jan. 8, 1719.

† 17 vi   Thomas, b. ——; m. Abigail Knowlton Mar. 7, 1729.

11   Benoni[3] (Selley), farmer, resided in Salisbury and Seabrook; m. 1st, 28 Aug., 1703, Elenor Getchell who d. June 28, 1735-6; 2d, 9 Oct., 1739, Rachel Tappan of Kensington, N. H. Children :

BY ELENOR:

18 i   Mehitable, b. Feb. 15, 1704; m. 6 Jan. 1726-7, Thos. Eaton, Salisbury.

19 ii   Elizabeth, b. Aug. 4, 1705; m. Jan. 4, 1727-8, Wm. Smith, Salisbury.

† 20 iii   Thomas, b. June 27, 1707; m. 1st, Eliz. Fowler, 2d, Lydia French.

21 iv   Martha, b. May 21, 1709; m. July 18, 1728, Thos. Merrill, Salisbury.

† 22 v   Samuel, b. Apr. 19, 1711; m. ——, Martha ——.

† 23 vi   Benjamin, b. (?) 1713; m. ——, Judith ——, d. 1765.

24 vii   Eleanor, b. Sept. 29, 1715; m. Mar 20, 1735-6, Bildad Dow, Salisbury.

25 viii   Sarah, b. Apr. 20, 1720; m. Mar. 8, 1737, David Fowler, Salisbury.

26 ix   Dorcas, b. June 26, 1725; m. ——, (?) Chris. Tappan.

BY RACHEL:

27 x   Mary, b. Mar. 8, 1740.

28 xi   Abagail, b. Feb. 9, 1742.

13   John[4] (Sellea) resided in Hampton until 1734-5, when he removed to Biddeford; m. Elizabeth E., dau. of John Glidden of Exeter; was a mill owner and farmer. Many of his descendants continue the mode of spelling the name Sellea. This name will be repeated and his children given.

15   Capt. Joseph[4] (Ceilley) of Hampton, m. Alice Rawlins of Exeter, in 1724-5; she was b. in 1701 and d. in 1801. Capt. Joseph moved to Nottingham, was one of the early settlers, a farmer, agent for the proprietors of the grant, and a captain of militia. Children :

29 i   Anna, b. (?) 1726; m. —— Mills; d. ——.

30 ii   Polly, b. ——; m. —— Sinclair; d. ——.

31 iii   Alice, b. —— ; m. 25 Oct., 1760, Enoch Page; d. ——.

† 32 iv   Joseph, b. — 1734; m. 4 Nov., 1756, Sarah Longfellow[c]; d. Aug., 1799.

---

[c]Jona. Longfellow, father of Sarah, was b. 23 May, 1714; m. Mercy Clark, 28 Oct., 1731; she was b. 26 Dec., 1714. Children: Stephen, b. July 19, 1733; Mary, b. 15 June, 1735; Jacob, b. 6 Nov., 1737; Sarah, b. 17 Nov., 1739; Elizabeth, b. 17 July, 1741; Nathan, b. 30 Dec., 1743; Anna, b. 15 Oct., 1745; Hannah, b. 1 Dec., 1747; Daniel, b. 16 Dec., 1749; David, b. 16 Dec., 1751; Enoch, b. 14 Aug., 1753; Jonathan, b. 28 April, 1756.

33　v　Abagail, b. — —; m. — —, Zephaniah Butler*; d. — —.
† 34　vi　Cutting, b. —, (?) 1738; m. —, (?) 1761, Martha Morrill; d. —, 1825.

17 Thomas⁴ (spelled his name Sillea) m. 7 Mar. 1729, Abagail Knowlton at Hampton Falls. In 1745 was a soldier in Colonel Moore's N. H. Regiment at Louisburg and present at its capture. His name appears with other soldiers in a petition to the Masonian proprietors in 1750, for a grant of a township (partly in consideration of their patriotic services) next north of Bakerstown, now Salisbury. The petition was granted, and he received three lots. The original document is now in the hands of George E. Emery of Lynn, Mass., one of his descendants. Thomas appears in the original plan of the Township of Andover, then New Brittan, and he gave Lot 22, East Div., 2d Range, to his son Jonathan Sillia, then a resident of Nottingham, N. H. Was with others a petitioner in 1739 for annexation to Massachusetts. Children :

35　i　Hannah, — —, Hampton Falls; m. —— Hilliard of Hampton Falls.
36　ii　Nancy, b. — —, Hampton Falls; m. —— Cass; moved to Sanbornton, N. H.
37　iii　Polly, b. — —, Hampton Falls; m —— Brown; moved to Epsom, N. H.
† 38　iv　Jonathan, b. 14 Sept., 1745, Hampton Falls; m. 1st Deborah Dearborn, 2d Mary Fellows, 3d Mrs. Williams.

20 Thomas⁴, b. 27 June, 1707; m. —, 1731, 1st, Elizabeth Fowler, who d. childless, 2d, Lydia French, in 1736, and had issue :

39　i　Jemima, b. 5 April, 1737,
† 40　ii　John, b. 14 Jan. 1739; m. 7 Nov., 1761, Elizabeth Fowler of Salisbury.
41　iii　Elizabeth, b. 1 Nov., 1740; m. 17 Oct., 1761, Jos. Flanders of Salisbury.
42　iv　Jane, b. 26 Nov., 1742.
43　v　Lydia, b. 12 Nov., 1744; m. 11 May, 1765, Thomas Evans of Salisbury.
† 44　vi　Jacob, b. 28 Feb., 1746; m. Anna ——.
45　vii　Judith, b. 10 Sept., 1748.

22 Samuel⁴, b. April 19, 1711 ; m. Martha ——. Children :

† 46　i　Benjamin, b. — —; m. a Miss Collins of Weare.
† 47　ii　Thomas, b. — —.
† 48　iii　Jonathan, b. — —; m. Hannah Greenleaf of Seabrook; d. Weare.
49　iv　Mehitable, b. — —; m. Winthrop Dow.
50　v　Elinor, b. 10 Aug., 1739; m. 7 Apr., 1757, Jno. Hunt of Salisbury.
51　vi　Mary, b. 31 Jan., 1741.

---

* Zephaniah was grandfather of Gen. Benjamin F. Butler.

23 Benjamin[4], b. — —; m. Judith ——; they lived in Salisbury, Kingston and Hawke, now Danville. He died in 1765, *vide* Prob. Rec., Rock. Co., vol. 1765–7, p. 152—a deposition. In a deed dated Jan. 6, 1770, Rock. Co. Rec., vol. 121, p. 274, mention is made of Judith Silley, widow, and the following children :

† 52 i   William, Gorumtown, Mass.
† 53 ii   John, Hawke, N. H.
† 54 iii   Benjamin, New Brittan, N. H.
† 55 iv   Moses, Salisbury, New Boston.
   56 v   Mary, m. Ebenezer Tucker, New Brittan, N. H.
† 57 vi   Samuel, Salisbury.
   58 vii · Elizabeth, m. Nathan Rowe, New Brittan, N. H.
† 59 viii Aaron, b. 1746; m. — —; d. 1805.

32 Gen. Joseph[5], b. in Nottingham ; farmer, town officer. He was engaged in the attack upon Fort William and Mary in 1774, and was among the zealous patriots of that day. Upon the news of the battle of Lexington, he marched for the scene of action at the head of one hundred volunteers from Nottingham and vicinity. He was appointed Major in Poor's (2d) Regiment by the Assembly of New Hampshire. As this regiment was engaged in home defense, he did not participate in the battle of the 17th June. He was made Lt. Col. in 1776, and April 2, 1777, was appointed Colonel of the 1st New Hampshire Regiment of three years' men, in the Continental Army, in place of Col. Stark, resigned. He fought his regiment bravely at Bemus Heights, was at the surrender of Burgoyne, storming of Stoney Point, Monmouth, and other hard fought battles of the Revolution.* After the war he was appointed Major General of the 1st Division of N. H. Militia, June 22, 1786, and as such headed the troops that quelled the insurrection of that year ; arresting the leader of the rebels in the midst of his armed followers, with his own hand. He was successively Treasurer, Vice President and President of the Order of Cincinnati in N. H ; a member of the Legislature and Councillor. Gen. Cilley was a man of great energy and industry ; of strong passions, yet generous and humane. He died in August, 1799, aged 64 years. Children :

---

* Saturday, March 19th, 1779, the N. H. Assembly voted unanimously, " that the worthy Col. Jos. Cilley be presented with a pair of pistols as a token of this State's good intention to reward merit in a brave officer."

60 i   Sarah, b. 16 Oct., 1757; m. 19 Aug., 1773, Judge Thomas Bartlett*; died Dec. 7, 1833.

61 ii   Bradbury, b. 1 Feb., 1760; m. 19 Nov., 1792, Martha, dau. of Gen. E. Poor. Hon. Bradbury Cilley was born in Nottingham. He was not much in public life, preferring the pursuits of a private citizen. He was elected a Representative to Congress in 1813, and served one term. In 1814 he was Colonel and appointed Aide on the Staff of Gov. Gilman of N. H., and served in that capacity two years, being on active duty in the fall of 1814. In 1817, was U. S. Marshal for the N. H. District. He was a man of large wealth, and died in Nottingham Dec. 17, 1831, in the 72d year of his age, without issue.

† 62 iii   Jonathan, b. 8 Mar., 1762; m. 5 July, 1786, Dorcas Butler; d. —— —.

63 iv   Joseph, b. 19 Nov., 1764; unmarried; d. 3 Dec , 1779.

† 64 v   Greenleaf, b 5 March, 1767; m. 22 May, 1788, Jennie Nealley; d. 25 Feb., 1803.

† 65 vi   Daniel, b. 12 Mar., 1769; m. 7 Nov., 1790, Hannah Plummer; d. 4 Dec., 1842.

66 vii   Elizabeth, b. 19 July, 1771; m. 3 April, 1791, Samuel Plummer; d. Dec. 8, 1809.

† 67 viii   Jacob, b. 19 July, 1773; m. 8 Jan., 1801, Harriet, dau. of Gen. E. Poor; d. 22 Jan., 1831.

68 ix   Anna, b. 22 May, 1775; m. 17 Apr., 1794, Nath'l Williams; d. 18 May, 1810.

† 69 x   Horatio Gates, b. 23 Dec , 1777; m. 17 Nov., 1802, Sally Jenness; d. 26 Nov., 1837.

34 Cutting[5], b. in Nottingham; was a farmer, town officer, and Captain during the Revolutionary War; d. at his son John's, in Northfield, in 1825.

† 70 i   Eliphalet, b. 30 Aug , 1762; m. —— —, Dolly Shaw; d. —— —.

71 ii   Joseph, b. 24 Sept., 1764; unmarried; d. at sea.

† 72 iii   John, b. 30 Sept., 1766; m. —— —, Hannah Elliot; d. Nov. 7, 1852.

73 iv   Elles, b. 27 Sept., 1768; m. (?) 1788, William Watson; d. 26 Mar., 1853.

---

*Israel Bartlett, b. 30 April, 1712; m. Lovy Alice Hall, b. June 10, 1716, on May 7, 1738. Brother of Josiah, the signer of Declaration of Independence. Children:

Jos. Hall, b. Mar. 7, 1739 o. s. Sarah, b. Nov. 25, 1741 id. Thomas, b. Oct. 22, 1745 id. Israel, b. May 8, 1748 id. Mary, b. Aug. 17, 1751 id. Josiah, b. Mar. 15, 1753 n. s.

Col. Thomas Bartlett m. Sarah Cilley Aug. 19, 1773. He was Captain of a company of "six-weeks'" men at Winter Hill in 1775, a Lt. Col. in Col. Gilman's Regt. in 1776, same in Col. Evans' Regt. in Rhode Island in 1778, and Col. of one of the N. H Regts. raised for the defense of West Point in 1780,—and member of Com. of Safety from May 28, 1778 to Jan. 5, 1779. Children:

Israel, b. 18 Jan , 1774; d. 28 April, 1859. Joseph, b. 22 Mar., 1776; d. at sea. Thomas, b. 24 Apr., 1778. d. 29 Sept., 1842. Jonathan, b. 2 July, 1780; d. —— —. Bradbury, b. 21 Jan., 1783; d. 1 Sept., 1869. Sarah, b. 26 July, 1785; d. 30 May, 1786. Josiah, b. 31 Mar., 1787; d. —— —. David, b. 29 April, 1769; d. —— —. Enoch, b. 6 July, 1791; d. 20 Dec., 1818. Betsey, b. 6 Aug., 1793; d. 3 Nov., 1845. Jacob, b. 16 June, 1796; d. 18 Feb , 1841. Patty Cilley, b. 7 Nov , 1798; d. 6 July, 1803.

74 v   Bradbury, b. 21 Mar., 1771; m. —— Burnham; moved East.

† 75 vi   Benjamin, b. 16 Apr., 1773; m. Unise Meader.

† 76 vii   Moses, b. 8 Feb., 1775; m. Susannah Barker.

† 77 viii   David, b. 26 Dec., 1776; m. —— Straw.

† 78 ix   Aaron, b. ——; m. 1st —— Yorke, 2d —— Yorke.

† 79 x   Henry, b. 27 Sept., 1785; m. Sally Sanborn; d. April 11, 1870.

80 xi   Betsey, b. ——; m. Aaron Page.

81 xii   Sally, b. ——; m. Eben Durgin; d. 10 Mar., 1875.

38 Jonathan (Sillia), b. at Hampton Falls; m. 1st, at Nottingham, Deborah, b. Feb. 5, 1743, dau. of Dea. Simon Dearborn of Epping, N. H., and sister of Gen. Henry Dearborn of Revolutionary fame. He moved from Nottingham to Andover about 1768. M. 2d, Mary, b. May 7, 1759, of Contoocook now Boscawen, dau. of Jos. Fellows, one of the first settlers in Andover. M. 3d, a Mrs. Williams of Grafton, N. H. Children:

BY FIRST WIFE:

82 i   Sarah, b. Aug. 6, 1770; m. — Nov., 1792, Willard Emery of Andover; d. at A. 12 Dec., 1847.

83 ii   Abagail,* b. 4 Jan., 1773; m. 17 Nov., 1796, Anthony Emery of Andover; d. at A. July 21, 1858.

84 iii   Polly, b. 11 Mar., 1775; m. John Fellows of Andover.

85 iv   Nancy, b. 9 June, 1779; m. Elijah Hilton of Andover.

† 86 v   Jonathan, b. 25 Dec , 1785; d. at Franklin, N. H.

BY SECOND WIFE:

87 vi   Deborah, b. 9 Jan., 1793; m. Ebenezer Tilton of Andover; d. in Illinois.

† 88 vii   Henry Dearborn, b. 10 Nov., 1794.

89 viii   Susannah, b. ——; m. Samuel Smith of Andover.

---

*Children of Abagail Cilley and Capt. Anthony Emery, son of Dr. Anthony Emery, who was in Col. Moore's N. H. Regt. at the capture of Louisburg:

i   John, b. Sept., 1797; d. at Andover, N. H., 16 Sept., 1805.

ii   Willard, b. 13 Mar., 1804; m. 13 Mar., 1825, Sarah Hobart; d. 21 July, 1871.

iii   John 2d, b. Oct., 1806; d. unmarried at Andover, 1871.

REFERENCES.

1. Rockingham Co. Rec., vol. ii, p. 47.   2. Same, vol. iii, p. 112; vol. iv, p. 26. 3. Same, vol. ii, p. 48.   4. Rock. Prob. Rec., vol. 1655-98, p. 91.   5. Rock. Court Rec., vol. 1685-87, p. 377.   6. Portsmouth Town Rec., vol. 1645-1713, p. 1.   7. Rock. Co. Rec., vol. xx, p. 54; vol. xxiii, p. 375.   8. Same, vol. xx, pp. 37, 447, 484. 9. Same, vol xxv, p. 462. *Ubi Supra.*

13 John[4]; issue (brought forward and now given).

28.1.   i   John Glidden, b. 8 May, 1726. Hamp. Falls records.

† 28.2 ii   Elijah, b. 19 Jan., 1740; m. —, Elizabeth Young, b. 1794; d 9 July, 1829.

† 28.3 iii Nathan, b 1 May, 1742; m. ——.

28.4   iv Abagail, b. 10 Jan., 1745; m. —— Knight, of Squam I.

28.2 Elijah[5] was lame; a schoolmaster; d. 26 Mar., 1821.

59.1   i   Phebe, b. ——; m. —— Guilford.   59.2 ii Olive, b. ——; d. young.

59 3 iii George, b. ——, pub. 20 Mar.,1798 to Mary Dearborn. s. p. d. —, 1820.

59.4 iv Hannah, b. ——; m. 11 Nov., 1809, Daniel Patterson; d. ——, 1849.

59.5 v   James, b. ——; m. 6 Mar., 1807, Jane Seavey. Served during the war of 1812 s. p. d. 1858.

59.6 vi Dama, b. —; d. infancy.   †59.7 vii Elijah, b —, m. Sally Ames; d. 1855.

28.3 Nathan[5], m. ——, d. 18 Aug., 1804.

59.8 i   Hannah, b. 3 Sept., 1766; m. ——, Philip Plaisted, Gorham, Me,

† 59.9 ii John, b. 27 Dec., 1767; m. ——, 1789, Lucy Phillips; d. 8 Aug , 1844.

59.10 iii Caleb (?)   59.11 iv A son (?)

38.1 Thomas (Selley[5]), b. —; m.—. Lived in Seabrook, and had issue. Sup. son of Thomas (20) by 1st wife.

90 i   Abagail, b. — —; m. — —, Jacob Fowler.

† 91 ii Thomas, b. — —; m. — —, Mercy Webber of Old York.

92 iii Richard, b ——(?); m. —, 1781, Susanna Panton (Sals Rec.).

93 iv Hannah, b. — —; unmarried.

40 John[5] m. Elizabeth Fowler of Salisbury (Sal. Rec.), and had :

† 94 i   Levi, b 23 May, 1772; m. 11 Nov., 1797, Abagail Hoyt.

† 95 ii Philip, b 1774; m. — —, Susan Whipple, b. —, 1774.

96 iii Mary, b. — —; m. — —, David Lull.

97 iv John, b. — —; m. — —, Mary Goodwin.

† 98 v   Aaron, b. — —; m. — —, Louise Murray of Hopkinton, N. H.

† 99 vi Seth Noble, b. 3 Dec., 1783; m. 23 May, 1813, Sarah Cavis; d. 27 May, 1861.

100 vii Lydia, b. — —; m. — —, Benjamin Marshal.

101 viii Thomas, b. — —, 1787; m. Mary Hoyt, b. — —, 1758.

102 ix Nancy, b. — —; m. — —, Thomas Colby.

44 Jacob[5] m. (?) 1769, Anna Whitcher. Lived in Weare, and died there or in Henniker, N. H., 1837 :

† 103 i   Amos, b. 27 Oct., 1770; m , 1st, 12 April, 1796, Elizabeth Blake; 2d, Ruth Nud, in Hampton, N. H.

104 ii   Nicholas, b. 18 Feb , 1774; m. 24 June 1799, Abagail Eaton of Seabrook.

† 105 iii David, b. 20 Feb., 1776; m. ——, Joanna Smith of Gilmantown.

† 106 iv Jacob, b 7 Jan., 1778; m. ——, Abagail Brown of Hampton.

107 v   Benjamin, b. ——; unmarried. Went to Ohio a young man and d.

† 108 vi Richard, b. March —, 1784; m ——, 1811, Betsey Swan, æ 24.

† 109 vii Joshua, b.—, 1786; m. —, 1809, Hannah Davie. b.—, 1787; d. 15 Feb. 1863.

2

† 110 viii   Enoch, b. ——; m. ——, Hannah Wallace of Henniker, N. H.

111 ix   John, b. ——; unmarried. Left Salisbury and was never heard from.

112 x

113 xi   Judith, b. ——; m. ——, Osgood Evans of E. Weare, and had: 1st, Col. Newell Seth, a trader, and Collector; 2nd, Olive C., m, ——, Moses Dearborn of S. Weare; 3d, Harrison, a trader, d.; 4th. Judith, unmarried; and 5th, Susan, m. ——, S. L. Fogg of Manchester, N. H.

114 xii   Nancy, b. ——; unmarried.

46 Benjamin[5], b. ——, 1744; m. 9 May, 1771, Elizabeth Edmonds of Salisbury, b. 1731 (Sals. Rec.); d. in Weare, N.H., —— 1811 or 12.

115 i   Polly, b. ——.   116 ii Betsey, b. ——.   117 iii Sally, b. ——.

† 118 iv   Benjamin, b. ——; m, 1st, ——, — Bean; 2d, ——.

† 119 v   Jonathan, b. 1776; m, ——, Lydia Eaton of Weare, b. 1770.

120 vi   Jenny D., b 1778.

47 Thomas[5], m. ——. Served during the Revolutionary war, and is said to have been in the battle of Bunker Hill. Was a U. S. pensioner.

† 121 i   Paul, b. ——; m. ——, — Collins of Weare.

122 ii   Thomas, b ——; m. ——, Flanders of Weare.

123 iii   Polly, b. ——; m. ——, — Greenleaf of Henniker.

124 iv   Betsey, b. ——; unmarried. Died in Weare.

125 v   Saul, b. ——; m. ——. Was a minister, and moved to Pennsylvania.

48 Jonathan[5], lived in Seabrook awhile; removed to Weare when young. He served as a private in Capt. Timothy Clements' company, Col. Pierce Long's regiment, N. H line, from August, 1776, to August, 1777, and was regularly discharged under the Continental establishment. His widow, Hannah, d. 7 Nov., 1842, he having d. 18 Jan., 1834.

† 126 i   Samuel, b. 16 March, 1789; m. ——, Hannah Eaton of Weare.

127 ii   Hannah, b. —April, 1787; m. ——, Abner Hunt of Seabrook.

† 128 iii   Winthrop, b. 17 June, 1789; m., 1st, Jemima Hadlock; 2d, ——, Canada; 3d, ——, Ohio.

† 129 iv   Jonathan, b 4 May, 1792; m., 1st, 26 Dec., 1816, Abagail Fowler of Seabrook; 2d, 19 Aug , 1855, Mary Jackman of Salisbury; No issue by 2d.

130 v   Betsey, b. ——, 1796; m. ——, John Graves of Andover.

131 vi   Jane, b. ——, 1798; m. ——, Winthrop Getchell of Weare.

52 William[5] (Selly), born ——, in Salisbury or Kingston, N. H. He enlisted April 11, 1758, and was discharged November 24, 1758. Served in Trueworthy Ladd's company (8th) of Exeter, in Col. John Hart's regiment, raised for the Crown Point expedition. A part joined the expedition against Louisburg, the remainder did service under Lieut. Col. Goffe, in the western part of N. H. He moved to Gorham, Maine, and m., ——, Anna Clark, b. 1 Sept., 1733. Removed to Buckfield, and d. in Brooks, ——, 1818. His name is mentioned in a deed in Rock. Co. Rec., vol. 121, p. 274, as a son of the late Benj. Selly of Salisbury, and as residing in Gorumtown, Mass., now Gorham, Me. Children :

† 132 i   John, b. ——: m. 15 Dec., 1786, Molly March.

† 133 ii   William, b. ——; m., 1st, 12 May, 1793, Sarah Bonney of Turner, d. 1837; 2d, ——, Miss — Waterhouse.

134 iii   Mary, b. ——, 1756; m. ——, Enoch Leathers of Sangerville.

135 iv   Abagail, b. ——; m. ——, Richard Knight.

136 v   Elizabeth, b ——; m. Benj. Skillings. Moved to Ohio.

† 137 vi   Benjamin, b. ——, 1758; m , 1st, 9 April, 1793, Patty Pearson of Bucktown; 2d, 22 Sept., 1803, Sally Newt of Buckfield; d 1842. *1846*

138 vii   Hannah, b. ——. m. 26 April, 1793, Caleb Lumber of Buckfield.

139 viii   Nelly, b. ——. m. ——, — Cluff.

140 ix   Fanny, } twins b. ——; m. 12 May, 1788, Joseph Lombard.
† 141 x   Ann, } b. ——; m. ——, Richard Lambert.

† 142 xi   Peter, b. ——, 1768; m. ——, 1800, Patty Tegro; d. 1855.

† 143 xii   Simon, b. ——, 1774; m. ——, Polly Teague; d. 1847.

53 John[5], m. 15 July, 1761, Abagail, daughter of John Clark and Elizabeth Clifford of Kingston, N. H. Lived awhile in Andover, N. H., and moved to Tunbridge, Vt., and died there the beginning of the present century. Issue :

† 144 i   Daniel, b. 1 March, 1762; m. ——, 1784, Anna Ellsworth, b. 5 August, 1758, d. 27 Feb., 1829; d. in Tunbridge, Vt.

145 ii   Judeth, b. 6 Dec., 1763.

† 146 iii   Benjamin, b. 14 October, 1765; m. 29 October, 1788, Sarah Wadleigh of Andover, N. H.

† 147 iv   Ebenezer, b. 28 Nov., 1767; m. ——, Polly Clement; died in Tunbridge, 12 December, 1848.

† 148 v   William, b. 27 October, 1769; m. 10 Sept , 1795, Abagail Ward; d in Jerico, Vt., 6 April, 1847.

149 vi   John, b. 2 April, 1772. Killed on a canal in New York.

† 150 vii   Jacob, b. 17 October, 1774; m., 1st, 7 January, 1790, Sally Chase, d ——, 1804; 2d, ——, 1805, Sally Cheney; d. in Tunbridge, 13 October, 1834.

151 viii   Moses, b. 25 Jan., 1777. Killed by a horse in Poultney, Vt , when a young man.

152 ix   Mary*, b. 24 March, 1779; m. 21 March, 1809, Joseph Buzzell; d. 7 March, 1864.

† 153 x   Satchel, b. 14 Feb., 1782; m. 16 Feb., 1809, Wealthy Cummings; d. 28 August, 1832. Settled in New York.

154 xi   Hannah, b. 2 August, 1784; m. ——, Robert Richardson.

155 xii   Clark, b. 12 July, 1786; m. ——. Settled in N. Y , or further west.

54 Benjamin[5] b. 12 May, 1742; m. 8 Oct., 1763, Apphia Kennison, who was b. 13 Nov., 1742, and d. 8 Nov., 1822. Lived in Brentwood, Poplin and Andover. Kept a tavern at Andover Center, which bore the name of Ben Affy's tavern; d. 9 Mar., 1804.

---

* Children of Joseph and Mary (Cilley) Buzzell: i, John C., b. 7 Jan., 1810; Phebe C., b. 8 Oct., 1812; Lydia S., b. 29 Nov., 1814; Abagail H M., b. 12 Dec., 1817; Otis C., b. 29 March, 1819; Elizabeth H., b. 2 July, 1821.

† 156 i   Elisha, b in Brentwood, 30 Apr., 1764; m. 10 Aug., 1786, Sally Keniston; d. 12 Feb., 1843.

† 157 ii   Benjamin, b. in Brentwood, 3 Sept., 1766; m. 23 July, 1790, Judith Cilley; d. 23 Mar., 1847.

† 158 iii   Philip, b. in Poplin, 13 Sept., 1768; m. 1789, Priscilla Keniston; d. 5 Nov., 1816.

159 iv   *Sarah, b. in Poplin, 25 Aug. 1771; m. 10 June, 1788, Jona. Keniston, b. 12 Feb., 1765, d. 5 June, 1834, bro. of Sally and Priscilla; d. 16 May. 1857.

† 160 v   Job, b. in Poplin, 3 May, 1775; m. 20 Sept., 1798, Susanna Seavy, b. 25 May, 1778, d. 23 March, 1876; d. 17 Feb., 1832.

† 161 vi   Stephen, b. in Poplin, 13 Oct , 1777; m. 29 ——, 1806, Abagail Currier; d. 18 May, 1844.

† 162 vii   William, b. in Andover, 13 July, 1780; m 21 Oct , 1801, Hannah Tucker, d. 19 Feb., 1852.

† 163 viii   Elijah, b. in Andover, 28 Dec., 1782; m. 3 Oct., 1804, Rhoda Keniston, cousin of Jona ; d. 31 May, 1826.

164 ix   Rebecca, b. 16 Sept., 1785; m. 28 Feb , 1809, John Wright.

55 Moses.[5]

165 i   Hannah, b. ——; m. ——, Moses French.

57 Deacon, Samuel[5] b.——m.——Betsey Springer.

166 i   Dolly, b. ——; m., 1st, 29 Oct , 1802, Nathaniel Ash; 2d, ——, Isaac Page.

167 ii   Sarah, b. ——; m. 4 Sept., 1828, Enoch W. George.

168 iii   Joseph, } twins, b.——. m. ——, Susan Springer, Sunnapee, N. H.
169 iv   Nancy, } b.——.

† 170 v   Samuel, b. 1753, m. 1st. Mary Blaisdell, issue.   2d. Hannah Parker, none. 3d. Ann Avery, issue.

171 vi ·   Charles, b. ——; m. 16 Oct., 1820, Betsey Mowe.

172 vii   Ruth, b. ——; m. 1 Jan , 1805 Stephen Sleeper.

173 viii   Elizabeth, b. ——; m. ——, William Conant.

174 ix   Bada P , b. ——; m. 13 Sept , 1824, John Morrill.

59 Aaron[5], b. 1746; m. —— Elizabeth Dodge, b. in Beverly, Mass., 1743; d Dec. 8, 1824. He built the first saw and grist mill in the west part of Andover, N. II., at the head of Blackwater river in 1795, now called Cilleyville. Issue :

175 i   Judith, b. ——; m. —— Benjamin Cilley.

† 176 ii   Benjamin, b. 1773; m. ——Sarah Wren, d. 1 May, 1846, æ. 67; d. 3 Mar. 1812

* Jona. Keniston and Sarah Cilley had: i Benjamin, b. 10 Sept , 1789; m. 10 Aug. 1812; d. 9 Sept , 1863. ii and iii (twins) Apphia and Sarah, b 15 April, 1791; d. — iv Apphia, b. 9 April, 1793; m. 15 Oct., 1812; d 10 Nov., 1876. v Sarah, b. 19 Feb. 1795; m —, 1826. vi Jonathan, b. 3 April, 1797; m 25 May, 1818; d. 22 July, 1873 vii William, b. 13 Feb., 1799; d. 11 Mar., 1853. viii Phillip, b. 10 April, 1801. ix Susanna, b. 8 April, 1803; d. —, —. x Rebecca, b. 4 March, 1809; m. 6 May, 1837; xi Elisha C., b. 21 Oct., 1807; m. 25 Dec , 1832. xii Polly M., b. 21 Dec., 1809; d. 16 Oct., 1829. xiii Lydia D , b. 18 June, 1812; m. 31 Jan., 1854.

† 177 iii   Edmund H., b. 1774; m. 11 May, 1802, Mehitable Wren, d. 18 Aug. 1834.

178 iv   Deborah, b. —— m. 11 Oct., 1792, Moses Tucker.

179 v   Betsey, b. —— m. —— Jonathan Tucker.

180 vi   Joanna, } twins, b 1780; m. 24, Aug., 1797, Henry Seavy.
181 vii   Jennie, }   b. 1780; m. ——, Green.

† 182 viii   Aaron, b. 5 June, 1782; m. 1st 8 Nov., 1803, Merriam Sleeper; 2d. 30 Jan., 1806, Lydia Currier; d. 24 July, 1863. *

† 183 ix   Jabish, b. 1786; m. 1st. Dolly Gove of Wilmot, 2d. 30 July, 1817, Mehitable Currier, d. 1855

59.7 Elijah,[6] (Silley.) Enlisted in the U. S. Navy during the war of 1812, and served on board the U. S. Ship of the Line, Washington. After the war, he settled in Daysville, Conn., m. —— Sally, dau. of Eliphalet and Alathea Ames-b. 29 Nov., 1799, d. Sept., 1874. He died in R. I., Feb. 1855.

184 i   Darius, b. 1828, d. 1823.

185 ii   Elizabeth, b. 1830, m. Ephriam Rice, d. 1858.

186 iii   Sarah, b. 1832, m. Henry Jinks, d. 1860.

† 187 iv   George, b. 11 Apr., 1835, m. 1st. 22d Aug. 1860, Mary A. Graffam, d. 10 Dec , 1871. 2d. 27 July, 1873, Sarah E. Holmes.

† 188 v   Willis, b. 4 July, 1837, m. 17 Apr., 1859, Elphronia Batchelder.

189 vi   Mary Ann, b. 17 June, 1822, m. 1st. 4 July, —— James J. Smith, had Edgar M., b. 9 Nov. 1850, Feanton, b. 7 May, 1852. Wm. E. , 2 Nov, 1854 2d. 1 May, 1865-Nathaniel Jinks.

190 vii   Lucy, b. ——, m. ——, George Roper.

191 viii ——.   192 ix——.   193 x——, died young.

59.9 John[6], (Sellea) was a sea captain, m. 1789, (?) Lucy Phillips, who was b. 18 Apr., 1769, and d. 21 Oct., 1842. Died in Saco, 8 Aug., 1844.

194 i   John, Jr., b. 9 Feb., 1790. Lost at sea, fell overboard.

195 ii   Sarah E., b. 18 Apr.. 1792, m. 27 Apr., 1817, Jno. Bryant Booth of Saco.

‡ 196 iii   Nathan, b. 25 Feb., 1794, m. 1817, Abigail Wormell of Thomaston, Me , d. Dec., 1822.

197 iv   Hannah, b. 21 May, 1795, m. 1821, Capt. Seth Spring of Hiram, d. 24 Mar., 1844, living.

† 198 v   Caleb, b. 27 Mar., 1799, m. —— Elizabeth D. Berry, d. 18 May, 1825.

† 199 vi   Barnard, b. 10 Sept , 1800; m. 14 Sept., 1802, Statira Burnham, d. 4 Dec, 1832.

† 200 vii   Joseph, b 31 Dec., 1801, m. 1st. 1 June 1826, Martha A. Gordon, d 22 Jan., 1833. 2d. 5 Jan., 1835, Mary J. Johnson, 3d—— living.

201 viii   Betsey, b. 31 Oct., 1803, m. 11 Nov. 1819, William S. Lowell. d.——

† 202 ix   Oliver, b. 26 Sept., 1805, m. ——, Hannah Hodgden, d 16 June, 1832.

† 203 x   Osman, b 5 Jan., 1809, m. Esther Hodgden, d. 1 July, 1837. d. ——

204 xi   Richard S., b. 18 Aug , 1810, m. ——, Elizabeth Hodgden,-had one dau., Hannah, who d. young. He served in the U. S. Navy, 1843 to 1845.

62 Jonathan[6], was born in Nottingham, N. H. When his father, Col. Cilley, marched from home, he took this son, then probably less than 15 years of age, with him. When the sudden march from Ticonderoga, took place, Jonathan was taken prisoner. As he was a mere boy, his captor learning who he was, took him to Gen. Burgoyne, who ordered that he should be treated kindly, and provided with a pass to join his father. He further ordered that he might select from the captured baggage of the American's (which was immense), any article of clothing he might desire. He therefore took the best looking coat he could find. It proved to have belonged to Major Hull, (afterwards the celebrated Gen. Hull). He was also provided with an old horse and pair of saddle-bags, filled with Burgoyne's proclamations, to convey to his father. On reaching the regiment, he found it on parade with his father in front. The Colonel seized one of the proclamations, and having read it, ordered them all to be torn to pieces, and said: "Thus may the British army be scattered!" I am unable to find the date of his enlistment, or his promotion to the rank of ensign, but in The Roll of the 1st. N. H. Line, dated Dec. 31, 1782, his name appears as lieutenant, with rank from May 11, 1782. He m. 5 June, 1786, Dorcas, dau. of Rev. Benj. and Dorcas (Abbott) Butler. He filled many town offices, was Justice of the Peace for Rock Co., Inspector and Brigade Major of the 3d. Brigade, Asst. Treasurer of the Order of Cincinnati, from 1794 to 1799, and Vice-President from 1799 to 1802.

In 1804, he moved with his family to near Cincinnati, Ohio. Mrs. Neff, one of his grandchildren, writes the following interesting incidents of his Western life:

" 'Twas told me when grand-father first arrived in the City of Cincinnati, he signed himself Jonathan Cilley, Gentleman, but was soon laughed out of it. Father told me Grand-mother's carriage was the first one ever drawn up the Cincinnati landing, that they all went down the Ohio from Wheeling on a flat boat, the only mode of conveyance at that time. He also told me, moving to the West killed his father, and would also his mother had she not been so hardy. I am reminded of an anecdote, how some of their rough neighbors called one evening as the family were seated around their fire, and demanded a table, light, and that room to play cards. Grand-father, as soon as he discovered their errand, pushed one of them to the wall by the throat and they were all glad to beat a retreat. This occured at Colerain, soon after he went there, probably to test his mettle. Why grand-father did not remain in the city I never knew. He purchased property in a valuable portion of the city, and had he retained it all, it would have been a large inheritance. Colerain was a fertile, healthy portion of the Miami valley and from the hills near the homestead, views for miles, agreeable and picturesque, were enjoyed. I suppose his large family, and perhaps a preference for the country took him there. It is said he desired to possess many acres of land. He died alone; was found in a field dead, and from appearance, it was supposed he had a fit of coughing, so violent, as to cause rupture a..d death. Of his military life, I have only heard he was sent out to take charge of the Newport barracks, opposite Cincinnati, but retained command only a short time; was sent out by President Jefferson.

As to appearances, I just remember at Colerian, a head, cut in paper and placed on black silk, framed, hanging on the wall, said to be a likeness of grand-father. The only thing that struck me as a child, was the queue. For years there has been at Mother's a crimson silk military scarf, with a sword, pistols and spurs, probably the same as mentioned in Gen Jos. Cilley's will, where he says, "My best sword and rigging; my pistols and holsters, and my military sash I give to my son Jonathan." Grand-mother's children were devoted to her and much harmony prevailed one with the other, they were clanish, ever reverting to their home and kinsfolks in New Hampshire.' "

205 i   Joseph, b. 28 Dec., 1786, unmarried. Served during the war of 1812, with great bravery, and was wounded. "He stepped upon a log and was urging his men forward by waving his sword. His prominent position attracted the attention of an Indian, who deliberately took aim at him and fired, the ball took effect in the arm that held the sword, but as his arm dropped, he caught the sword with his left hand and continued to rally and cheer his men." d. 28 Nov , 1828.

206 ii   Sarah, b. 7 Jan , 1789, m. 1st. ——, Rev. Hugh Andrews, and had issue: Harriet, Jonathan, Eliza, Amanda, Dorcas and Joseph Hugh m. 2d. Maj. Arthur Henry, —— d. 5 Oct. 1862.

† 207 iii   Benjamin, b. 7 Jan., 1789, m. —— Martha McCormick, d. 11 Feb , 1851.

† 208 iv   Jonathan, b 5 Jan., 1791, m. 24 Oct , 1830, Sarah Lee, d. 29 Dec., 1874.

209 v   Dorcas, b. 22 Sept., 1793, m. 1st. Uzzal Gould. 2d. — June, 1834, Sam'l Milliken, s. p. d. 7 June., 1837.

210 vi   Henry, b. 16 Apr., 1796, unmarried, d. 23 Mar., 1845.

† 211 vii   Bradbury, b. 16 May, 1798, m. 15 Feb. 1834, Harriet Hedges, d. 19 July, 1874.

212 viii   Mary, b. 25 May, 1800, m. 12 Nov., 1820, Sam'l Davis, and had issue : Bradbury Cilley, b. 19 Jan., 1831, d. 10 Oct., 1854.-Hester P. b 9 Oct , 1832, m. 6 Oct., 1857. J. P. Waterhouse, M.D., d. 30 Aug 1861.

213 ix   Martha Poor, b. 4 July, 1803, m. Feb., 1835, Phillip Brown, s. p. d. 23 Oct. 1848

214 x   Jacob, ⎫ Twins.
215 xi   Gates, ⎭ b. Jan., 1807. Both died young.

64 Greenleaf,' b. in Nottingham, m. Jennie, dau. of Joseph and Susanna (Bowdoin) Nealley of Lee, N. H. She was b. 22 Sept., 1772, d. 26 Mar., 1866.

He resided in Nottingham, was a farmer, Major in the State Miltia, and held at various times different town offices, d. 25 Feb., 1808.

His wife, writes one of her grand-children, had a very pleasant blue eye, and was a very intelligent woman. Married when 15 years of age, raised a large family and retained her sight, hearing and mental powers till the full age of 94 years.

To the very last she maintained her interest in all her children and grand-children and knew intimately the affairs of each, so that visits to her after years of absence would find her fully informed and prepared to converse with them on any part of their lives during the absence. She seemed short and was considerably bowed down with the weight of years. but her voice, eye, and hearing showed little diminution of power till the very day of her death. After she was 90, she made a bed-quilt for each one of her grand-daughters. She was never but once sick, and occupied her accustomed place at the fireside and table, till the day before her death, when she quietly remarked, as they prepared a bed for her down stairs, that she desired no change to be made, as she should need a bed but a day or two.

216 i Susanna, b. 8 Oct., 1788, m, 14 Feb., 1816, David Bartlett, b. 27 Apr., 1737, d. 27 July, 1868, and had, i. Jane, b. 10 Sept., 1816, d. 21 Dec., 1818 ii, Greenleaf Cilley, b. 7 May., 1822, m. 4 May, 1854, Charlotte J Kelley. had Frederick D. b. 16 Mar., 1855, d. 21 March, 1877, Greenleaf K. b. 17 June 1856, Charles, b. 9 Apr., 1859, William, b. 24 Feb , 1862, Jennie S., b. 25 March, 1864. iii Jonathan, b. 11 March, 1824, d 29 July., 1828. iv David Frederick, b. 15 May, 1827, m. 27 Oct , 1857, Lawra A Towle, issue : Emma, J., b. 13 May, 1861 ; Susie H. b. 20, May, 1865.; Lizzie A , b., 13 July, 1868 ; May B , b. 25 Oct., 1875. Susanna, d. 10 Dec., 1858.

† 217 ii Joseph, b. 4 Jan , 1791, m. 15 Dec., 1824, Elizabeth Williams, living.

218 iii Greenleaf, b. 10 Jan., 1793, d. 11 Dec., 1811.

219 iv Frederick Augustus, b 28 Oct., 1796, ——, d. 6 Oct., 1815.

220 v Sarah Longfellow, b. 14 Aug., 1799, m. 4 Dec., 1827, Abram Plumer, and had i. Sarah Jane, b. 11 Oct , 1828, d 3 Aug., 1859. ii Greenleaf Bradbury, b. 22 May, 1830, d. in California, 22 May, 1858. iii. Bradbury Greenleaf, b. 22 May, 1830, living in Warsaw, Wis. iv. Elizabeth Ann, b. 1 Feb., 1832, m. 7 Dec 1865, Caleb F. Edgerly of Epping, and have Sarah Jane, b. 5 Nov., 1866, and Joseph Abraham, b. 15 May, 1873. v. Daniel Longfellow, b. 3. July, 1837, m. 13 Sept., 1869, Mary Jane Draper, living in Warsaw, Wisconsin. vi. Joseph Abraham, b. 8 June, 1840. vii. James Shrigley, Ord. Serg't 11, N.H. Inf., killed at Fredericksburg, 13 Dec. 1862. Living.

† 221 vi Jonathan, b. 2 July, 1802, m. 4 Apr., 1829, Deborah Prince, d. 24 Feb., 1838.

222 vii Elizabeth Ann, b. 11 July, 1804, m. 7 Nov. 1826, Benj. Burley of Epping, N. H., aud had, i. Joseph Cilley, b. 13 Jan., 1830, m. 17 Dec. 1855, Sarah E., dau. of Sam'l and Sally (Bartlett) Haley of Epping, N H., and have Nannie, b., 5 Oct., 1857, Harry Benj , b. 26 May, 1867, Alice, b. 23 Sept., 1870, Jennie Cilley, b. 10 Sept 1872, Benj. Thomas b. 26 Nov , 1874. ii. Nannie J., b. 21 Nov., 1832, d. 5 Oct., 1855. Mrs. Burley d. 5 Oct., 1876.

65 Daniel[6], m. 7 Nov., 1790, Harriet, dau. of Samuel and Mary (Dole) Plumer, and sister of the late Gov. Wm. Plumer of N. H. She d. 19th Feb., 1850.

* 223 i Polly Dole, b. 11 May, 1791; m. ——, Robert Knox; d. 27 May, 1844.

224 ii Bradbury, b 8 May, 1793; m., 1st, Sally Wiggin; 2d, Mary Smith. No issue. Died 22 March, 1872.

† 225 iii Samuel P., b. 12 October, 1795; m. 2 Dec., 1827, Hannah W. Critchett of Epsom; d. 21 June, 1875.

226 iv Joseph, b. 20 June, 1797; ——; d. 5 May, 1806.

227 v Daniel, b. 19 April, 1804; ——; d. 10 Jan., 1806.

† 228 vi Daniel Plumer, b. 31 May, 1806; m. 13 Jan., 1836, Adelaide Ayres Haines.

229 vii Hannah Plumer, b. 31 May, 1806; ——; d. 28 June, 1826.

† 230 viii William P., b. 24 Nov , 1808; m., 1st, 11 Feb , 1834, Emeline Whitney; 2d 20 Nov., 1862, Mrs. Nancy J. Dudley.

† 231 ix Jonathan L., b. 24 Nov , 1808; m. ——, Harriet Whitney.

67 Jacob[6] m. Harriet, daughter of Gen. Enoch Poor. She was b. 31 Jan., 1780, and d. 7 June, 1838. He served as Major in the militia, Civil Magistrate, and held many town offices at different periods, and was member of the State Legislature in 1802-3-6-7-8-10-12-13. Died 29 Jan., 1831.

232 i Enoch Poor, b 17 Oct., 1801; unmarried; d. 25 Dec , 1820.

† 233 ii Joseph Longfellow, b. 27 Oct., 1803; m. 22 Nov., 1837, Lavinia B. Kelley; d. 18 August, 1868.

† 234 iii John Osgood, b. 12 Feb., 1809; m. 23 Oct., 1832, Henrietta Butler

235 iv Harriet Poor, b. 22 Sept., 1811; m. 6 Sept., 1841, Rev. T. G Brainherd, and had : i Harriet Poor, b. 9 Sept., 1842; ii Julia Dana, b. 24 Nov., 1843; iii Henry Hungerford, b 31 Jan., 1845, d 5 Feb., 1848; iv Martha Cilley, b. 12 Nov., 1846; v Hannah Hungerford, b. 22 Sept., 1848. Died 22 Sept., 1848.

† 236 v Jacob Green, b. 6 April, 1817; m. 1st, ——, 1845, Emma Stark; 2d, 29 Jan., 1861, Martha Cilley Bouton; d. 7 Sept., 1870.

237 vi Martha Osgood, b. 11 Jan., 1819; m. 16 Feb., 1846, F. B. Berry.

† 238 vii Bradbury Poor, b. 2 Jan., 1824; m. 30 June, 1856, Angeline Baldwin.

---

* Polly Dole Cilley m. ——, Robert Knox, and d. 1844. Issue: i Mary Dole Cilley, b 15 Sept., 1815, m. 13 July, 1837, Hon. Asa Fowler of Concord, N. H., son of Benj. and Mehitable (Ladd) Fowler, b. 23 Feb., 1811. Issue: Frank Asa, b. 24 May, 1842; Geo. Robert, b. 25 April, 1844, m. Isabel, dau. of Hon. Josiah and Abbie Haynes Minot of Concord, N. H.; Clara Maria, b. 3 June, 1847; Wm. Plumer, b. 3 Oct., 1850; and Edward Cilley, b. 11 Jan., 1853, m. ——, Sarah Watson, resides in Boston.

69 Horatio Gates[6]; b. in Nottingham, m. 17 Nov., 1802, Sally Jenness of Deerfield, who was b. 4 Aug., 1782, and d. 11 Nov., 1865. He lived in Deerfield, and was a man of great energy of character, a safe counsellor, good advocate, generous and humane. Died 26 Nov., 1837. Issue :

239 i   A daughter, b. 30 Jan, 1804, lived but a few hours.

† 240 ii   Horatio Gates, b. 25 Nov. 1805, m. May, 1840, Deborah Jenness, d. 13 Mar., 1874.

241 iii   Sally Jenness, b. 2 Nov., 1807, m ——, d. 15 Apr., 1826.

242 iv   Elizabeth Ann, b 30 Aug, 1810, m. Feb 1840, Rev. N. Bouton, D. D., of Concord, N. H. State Historian for the last 10 years. Their children : 1st. Sarah Cilley, m. Gen. J. N. Patterson, grad. of Dartmouth and who served 4 years and 9 mos in 2nd. N. H. Inf., during the war of the rebellion; they have three children. 2d. Martha Cilley, m. J. G. Cilley. 3d. Jennie Louise.

243 v   Martha Osgood, b. 24 May, 1814, resides at South Deerfield.

244 vi   Mary Jane, b. 5 June, 1816, m 5 Oct. 1842, Ephraim Eaton, lawyer, and graduate of Dartmouth College. Had Mary Jane and Henry.

245 vii Joseph Bradbury, b. 30 Jan., 1819, ——, d. 16 Feb., 1823.

246 viii Harriet Newell, b. 27 Oct., 1822. ——, d. 9 Jan , 1838.

† 247 ix Joseph Bradbury, b 26 Dec., 1824, m 11 Nov. 1847, Elizabeth Jenness, d. 23 Nov., 1872.

70 Eliphalet[6], a farmer. Resided in Nottingham and Epping.

248 i   Alice, b. 5 Oct., 1788, m. ——, Neal of Newmarket.

249 ii   Samuel, b. 2 Aug., 1790, unmarried, was serg't in 21st Reg't, and died in the war of 1812, at Platsburg, N. Y. His heirs received his land warrant.

† 250 iii Joseph, b. 27 Sept. 1793, pub. 23 Feb , 1822, Nancy Maloon, d. Apr., 1867.

251 iv   Abagail, b. 2 June, 1796, m. ——, Bean of Candia

252 v   Jonathan, b. 4 Nov 1790, unmarried, d. in Charlestown, Mass.

253 vi   George, b ——, d. in New York.

72 John[6], b. in Nottingham, moved to Northfield, m. 21 Dec., 1786, Hannah Elliott, who was b Mar., 4, 1768, and d. 10 Oct., 1852, dau. of John Elliott of Epping, N. H. He d. 7 Nov., 1852.

254 i   Polly E b. 4 Mar , 1786, m. ——, Jacob Webber, b. ——, 1780, d 25 Aug., 1857.

255 ii   Joseph, b. 29 Dec., 1789 m ——, d. 28 March, 1800.

256 iii Martha B., b. 29 Apr., 1791, m. ——, Jesse Rogers, b. 28 Mar., 1787, d. 4 Aug., 1852, d. 10 June, 1867.

† 257 iv John Jr., b 25 Mar., 1793, m. 1st. ——, Betsey Hill, 2nd. ——, Lucy Blodgett, living.

† 258 v   Abraham B., b. 12 March, 1795, m. 25 May, 1814, Rebecca Dow, b. 10 Jan., 1796, d 22 Mar., 1873, d. 5 Apr 1875.

† 259 vi Sewall, b 30 Mar. 1797, m. ——, 1820, Rebecca Miers, she was b. 31 Oct , 1799, he died 6 Apr. 1874.

260 vii Lydia, b. 8 July, 1798, m. ——, d. 8 Jan'y, 1800.

† 261 viii Jonathan E., b. 24 July, 1800, m. 1st. Elizabeth C. Taylor, b. 8 Mar. 1808,
        d. 4. March, 1848. 2d. Lucinda Burbank, b. 16 June, 1812. Living.

262 ix Naomi E., b. 24 Apr. 1802, m. ——, 1834, Geo. W. Currier, who was b.
        July 13, 1814.

† 263 x Daniel E., b. 3 May, 1804, m. 1st. 20 Dec. 1827, Betsy P. Cilley. 2nd. 5
        Nov. 1863, Martha Burnham, b. 19 Aug., 1832.

† 264 xi James C., b. 23 March, 1806, m. 10 May, 1827, Irena S. Rand, lives in
        Belmont, N. H.

265 xii Sophronia, b. 27 July, 1808, ——, d. 1 Aug. 1808.

† 266 xiii Hiram, b. 27 July, 1810, m 28 Jan. 1830, Nancy G. Kimball, b 10 Dec.,
        1813.

267 xiv William P., b. 30 March, 1813, killed by a falling tree, Nov. 8, 1825,

74 Bradbury,[6] b. in Nottingham, m. 1801, Susan Straw, moved to Newfield, Me., was a Major in militia. d. 5 Sept. 1832.

268 i Kitty, b. 1802, m. ——, Wm. Dunnels of Newfield, and had Zachariah, Ag-
        nes, Armind, Abial, John, Aaron, Catherine, Caleb, Susan Morrell.

269 ii Betsy, b. 1804, m. ——, Silas Durgin of Limerick, Me., and had Frederick,
        Bradbury C., Silas, Caleb, Alonzo, Munroe, Henry, Frank.

270 iii Mary, b. 1806, m. ——, Dan'l Heath of Shapleigh, and had Rufus Wil-
        liam, Mary Jane, Eliza Ann, Matilda E., Charles E.

271 iv Susan, b, 1808, d. s p.

272 v Louisa, b. 1812, m. ——, Sam'l Cole of Saco, s. p. d. 3 Aug., 1842.

273 vi Harriet Newell, b. 28 Oct., 1816, m. 18 Aug. 1835, Obadiah T Guptill, of
        Saco, Me., and had, i. Ferdinand W , b. 7 Mar., 1837, now a lawyer
        and Deputy Collector of Customs of Saco, Me. ii. Clara Augusta, b.
        11 Feb. 1839, lives in Biddeford. iii Ira Clark, lives in Kennebunk.

75 Benjamin,[6] b. in Nottingham, m. Eunice Meader.

274 i Abigail, b. 10 July, 1795, m. —— Chandler.

275 ii Nancy Williams, b. 16, Dec., 1797.

276 iii Joseph Freeman, b. 16 Dec , 1801, lives in Epson, N. H. No issue.

277 iv Maria, b. 19 March, 1805.

278 v Elvina, b. 13 Apr., 1811.

76 Moses[6], after called Morgan, was b. and resided in Nottingham, a farmer, m. 1st. 29 Sept. 1793, Susanna Barker. 2d. 20 Oct 1831, Olive Blaisdell.

279 i Cutting 2d., b. 28 Jan., 1794.

280 ii Moses, b. 3 June, 1797. 281 iii Jacob, b. 1 Dec. 1801. 282 iv Jotham
        Ringe Roger, b 13 Apr. 1806. 283, v Chandler, b. 29 Mar., 1808.
        284 vi William Guy, b. 7 May, 1810. 285 vii Gardner, b. 1 May,
        1812. They all died young.

77 David[6], b. 26 Dec., 1776, in Nottingham, m. 16 Jan., 1798 Polly Straw of Epping.

286 i Martha, b. ——, m. ——, Greenleaf Emerson.

287 ii Joseph, b. ——, m. ——, Burnham, and had children, but all died young.

78 Aaron⁶, b. 10 Dec., 1781, m. 1st. Mary York, 2d. Polly York, 3d. April 1838, Mrs. Mary Randall of Northwood.

288 i   Samuel, b. 10 Nov , 1803.

289 ii   John, b. 9 Sept. 1804, m. Betsey Brown, d. 12 Dec., 1875.

290 iii   Abigail, b. 10 Apr., 1810, m. Dec. 1831, Rufus Roberts.

† 291 iv   Joseph Shephard, b. 11 Oct., 1818, m. 1845, Mahala A. Evans, lives in North-
        wood.

79 Henry⁶, b. ——, m. 23 Nov., 1809, Sally Sanborn.

292 i   Betsy P. b. 25 March, 1810, m. 20 Dec., 1827, Dan'l E. Cilley, d. 13 Feb.,
        1862.

293 ii   Samuel, b. 19 Aug., 1813, unmarried, d. in S. Newmarket.

294 iii   Jonathan S., b. 2 Feb., 1818, m. ——, Ann Blaisdell, no issue.

86 Jonathan⁶, (Celley) b. 25 Dec., 1786, m. Jan. 1808, Betsy Hilton of Andover, d. in Franklin, N. H., 15 Oct., 1872.

295 i   Mary, b. 24 May, 1810, m. 10 Sept., 1832, Alvah Buzzell of Parsonville,
        Me., d. 17 May, 1865.

296 ii   Abagail, b. 16 May, 1812. ——, d. 15 June, 1836.

† 297 iii   Henry Dearborn, b. 20 June, 1814, m. 12 Apr., 1840, Susan F. Fuller, of
        Andover, N. H.

298 iv   Sally H., b. 17 Dec , 1816, m. 18 Mar., 1848, Wm. Proctor, of Franklin,
        N. H., and had George, Warren and Mary Jane.

88 Henry Dearborn⁶, b. 10 Nov., 1795, m. May, 1823, Susan Sanborn, d. 30 Jan., 1844.

† 299 i   Jonathan, b. 10 Jan., 1825, m. 1 Jan. 1852, Elizabeth Wall.

300 ii   Mary, b. ——, d. in Andover.

?01 iii   William H., b. 15 Mar., 1835, unmarried.

91 Thomas⁶, (Selley) b. ——, m. ——, Mercy Webber of Old York, lived in Seabrook, served in the war of 1812.

302 i   Dolly, b. ——, m. 27 Feb., 1815, David Bagley.

† 303 ii   James, b. 24 Mar , 1793, m 1st. 29 Nov. 1818, Elizabeth Rowe, b. 1785, d.
        1848. 2d. ——, Lavinia Mc Donnell, living, Kensington.

304 iii   Lydia, b. ——, unmarried.

305 iv   Edwin, b. ——, m. ——, Mirriam Dow, had twins, both d. young.

† 306 v   Mark, b. ——, m. ——, Mary Dow.

307 vi   Maria, b. ——, m 1st. —— Nehemiah Brown,2nd. —— John Kilburn.

† 308 vii   William, b.   — m. 1st. Betsey Brown, 2nd. Wright.

309 viii   Washington, b. ——, unmarried.

310 ix   Betsy, b. 22 Dec. 1812, m. 1827, James Johnson, living in Seabrook.

311 x   Susan, b. "   "   " m. 1st. 9 Jan. 1837, Nathan Kilburn. 2d. Benj.
        Howard.

94 Levi⁶, had:

† 312 i   Amos Wood, b. 8 June, 1798, m. ——, Mehitable Melvin, d. July, 1869.

† 313 ii   John, b. 20 Sept., 1801, m. ——Judith Cilley, d. 20 Sept. 1854.

† 314 iii   Ambrose Chase, b. 11 June, 1803, m. ——, Ruth M. Eaton, d. 11 June, 1833.

315 iv Abagail H., b. 10 March, 1805, m. David T. Straw, living in E Weare.

316 v Elizabeth, b. 12 Nov 1811, unmarried, d. 14 Nov. 1833.

317 vi Benjamin H., b. 24 Oct., 1813, unmarried, ——, d. 27 Nov. 1840.

† 318 vii Joseph Worthen, b. 28 June, 1817, m. 4 Feb., 1840, Lydia Bartlett, living in Weare.

95 Phillip⁶, b. 1774, m. Susan Whipple, b. 1774. Was a physician.

319 i Elbridge. 320 ii ——. 321 iii ——. 322 iv ——. 323 v ——.

97 John⁶, b. ——, m.——, Mary Goodwin.

324 i ——. 325 ii ——.

98 Aaron⁶, b. ——, m. ——, Louisa Murray. Kept a hotel in Goffstown, N. H. and Bucksport, Me.; afterwards, went into trade at Bucksport.

326 i Maria Sibley, b. 12 July, 1801 in Hopkinton, N. H.

327 ii Sophronia, b. 13 Dec., 1802 in Weare, N. H.

328 iii Elizabeth Fowler, b. 11 Aug., 1806 in Weare, N.H., living in Bucksport Me.

329 iv Leander, b. 17 Apr., 1808, in Weare, N. H.

330 v George Washington, b. 28 Jan., 1813, in Bucksport, Me.

331 vi —— 332 vii ——

99 Seth Noble⁶, m. Sarah dau. of ·—— Cavis, was a farmer, represented his town for three years in the State Legislature, held various town offices.

† 333 i John C., b 10 March, 1814; m. 1st, 18 Sept., 1850, Patience Martin; 2d, 30 June, 1859, Lydia Whitaker.

334 ii Elizabeth L., b. 9 June, 1815; m. 10 Oct., 1839, Hon. John L. Hadley of S. Weare, Secretary of State for many years. Issue: George L., Mary Louise, Charles John, Sarah Mehitable and Henry Philip.

335 iii Mary A., b. 31 Jan., 1817; m. 15 March, 1847, Nathan McCoy of S. Weare. Had issue: James Noble, b. 11 Dec., 1848; m. 1st, 1 Dec , 1868, Alice Cornelia Andrews of Cedar Rapids, Iowa; 2d, 1 Dec., 1873, Alice Frothingham Edmunds of Hopkinton, Vt , and they have: Alice Cornelia, b. 24 April, 1875.

336 iv Philip Noble, b. 9 March, 1821; m. 1st, 23 April, 1851, Caroline Sarah Safford; 2d, 14 April, 1859, Sarah Karb Whitman.

101 Thomas. b. ——, 1787, m. Mary Hoyt, b. 1758.

337 i——; 338 ii ——; 339 iii ——; 340 iv ——; 341 v ——.

103 Amos⁶, ——, m. 1st. Elizabeth Blake, 2d. Ruth Nud of Hampton, N. H.

BY FIRST WIFE:

342 i Oliver, b. ——; d. in Havana, W. I., of yellow fever.

343 ii Betsey, b ——; dead.

344 iii Amos, b. ——; died in Boston.

BY SECOND WIFE:

† 345 iv Justin, b. ——; m. 1 April, 1831, Mary Ann ——; d. 16 Sept., 1862.

† 346 v   William, b. 7 Oct., 1817; m. 1st, — May, 1846, Lauretta E. Piper; 2d, 9
              Nov., 1858, Elizabeth A. Gerry.

347 vi   John,   died young.

348 vii Mary,   "   "

349 viii Oliver, "   "

104 Nicholas⁶, ——, m. 24 June, 1799, Abagail Eaton of Seabrook.

350 i —— . 351 ii —— 352 iii —— . 353 iv —— 354 v —— .

105 David⁶, ——, m. —— Joanna Smith of Gilmantown. He
resided there.

355 i   William, b. ——

356 ii Nancy b. ——, m. ——, Eliphalet F. Gilman of Gilmantown, and had Betsy
       Ann and Charlotte, both dead.

357 iii Alfred, b. ——, d. young.

358 iv Hannah, b. ——, 359 v Stratton, b. ——. 360 vi David, b. ——, unmar-
       ried and d.

361 vii Mary Ann, b. ——, m. ——, Bradley of Vt.

106 Jacob⁶, m. Abagail Brown of Hampton Falls, N. H., d.
May 1851, was a sailor and resided a while in Pittsfield, N. H., in
1825, moved to Atkinson, Me., d, 24 Mar., 1864.

† 362 i   Jonathan F., b. 24 Feb., 1801, m. 23 Jan , 1823, Mehitable Hilliard.

† 363 ii Isaac B., b. 4 Oct., 1804, m. ——, Betsy Blake.

†.364 iii Daniel C., b. 8 Sept., 1806, m. 23 Oct., 1828, Abagail Blake, d. 24 Aug.,
       1873.

365 iv Benj. S., b. 1809, m. 1st. ——, Susan Moulton of Sebec. 2d. —— Anna
       Glidden, s. p.

366 v   Jacob, b. 29 Dec., 1811, m. 25 Sept., 1837, Frances Adams, of N. H., s. p.
       d. 21 Jan., 1850.

367 vi Jemima A , b. 4. Oct., 1815, m. 25 Nov., 1840, Jos. M. Batchelder of Dover
       Me., a member of Co. G., 1st. Me Heavy Art'y, lost an arm and
       otherwise injured, before Petersburg, June 18, 1864.

368 vii Eliza J., b. 18 June, 1817, m. 25 May, 1840, Alson L. Cary of Bradford,
       Me.

108 Joshua⁶, b. in Seabrook, N. H., m. Hannah Davie of
New London, N. H., b. 1784, he d. 15 Feb. 1863.

369 i   Josiah, b. ——1810, ——, d. in infancy.

† 370 ii Richard, b. 4 Jan., 1812, m. ——, 1842, Desire Tubbs of Deering, N. H.

371 iii Mabala, b. Jan., 1814, ——, m. Arthur L. Clifford.

372 iv Lorenzo, b. July, 1816, m. ——, Ruth Flanders.

373 v   Adeline, b. Jan., 1818, ——, d. 1832.

374 vi Florilla, b. Jan., 1820, m. ——, John Ryder.

375 vii Hannah, b. ——, 1822, m. ——, Geo. Emerson, d. ——, 1876.

376 viii Nancy, b. ——, 1824, m. ——, Wm. A. Hill.

377 ix   Charlotte, b. ——, 1826, m. ——, Amos S. George.
378 x   Josiah D., b. March, 1831, m. ——. Lucy Kimball.

109   Richard[6], b. March, 1784, ——, m. 1811, Betsy Swan, æ. 24. Moved to Gilmantown, N. H., back to Weare, clothier for two years, thence to Concord, as a farmer, and in Sept., 1826, moved to Underhill, Vt., where he died, 28 Nov., 1855. His wife d. at Brandon, Vt , 16 Dec., 1870.

379 i   Eliza, b. 17 Aug., 1811, m. Jan., 1829, —— Howe, d. 4 July, 1840.
380 ii   Emily, b. 12 Mar , 1813, m. ——, d. 14 May, 1844.
† 381 iii Joseph S , b. 21 March, 1815, m. 28 May, 1840, Albina Crane.
† 382 iv   Walter H., b. 28 Nov., 1821, m. 26 Apr., 1846

110   Enoch[6], b. ——, m.——, Hannah Wallace of Henniker, lived in Weare, and E. Deering; was a school-master.

383 i   Wallace, b. ——, unmarried, lives in E. Deering, N. H.
384 ii   Mary Ann, b. ——, m.——, Capt. Quint, of Keene, N. H., d. ——.

118   Benjamin,[6] b. ——, m. 1st., —— Bean. 2d.——

385 i   Moses, 386 ii Madison, 387 iii Benjamin, 388 iv Ezra, 389 v Munroe: b.-——

119   Jonathan[6], b.——, m.——, Lydia Eaton of Weare, lived the latter part of his life in Manchester, N. H.

390 i   Judith, b. 1802, m.——, John Cilley. (313)
391 ii   Ruth, b. 1804, m.——, Moses Johnson of Weare.
392 iii   Avila, b. ——, m. ——, Berry of Pittsfield.
393 iv   Albert, b. 1806. 394 v Benjamin, b. 1808. 395 vi Tristam, b. 1812. 396
          vii Alfred, b 1830.
397 viii Lydia, b. 1811, unmarried.
398 ix   Eliza Jane, b. 1815, unmarried.
399 x   Harriet, b. 1837   "

121   Paul[6], b.——, m. ——, Collins of Weare.
† 400 i   Simmons B., b. 10 Jan., 1798, m. ——, Mary Parker Ayer, d. 18 Nov. 1870.
401 ii   Benjamin, b. ——
402 iii   Charles, b. ——   Bridgewater, Vt.
403 iv   Sally, b. ——
404 v   Thomas, b. ——
405 vi   Samuel, b.——
406 vii   Mary, b.——, m. ——, Messer of Methuen.
407 viii Eliza, b. ——, m. ——, Bragg of Lowell.
408 ix   Sarah, b. ——, m. ——, Flanders of Henniker.
† 409 x   Jonathan, b. ——, m. ——,   "   "   "
410 x   Jane, b. ——, m. ——, Moses Marshall of Canaan.

122   Thomas[6], b. ——, m. ——, Flanders of Weare.
411 i   ——. 412 ii ——. 413 iii ——.

125   Saul[6], b. ——, m. ——.   Went to Pennsylvania, a minister.
414 i   ——. 415 ii ——. 416 iii ——. 417 iv ——.

126 Samuel[6], b. 16 March, 1785, m. ——, Hannah Eaton of Weare.

418 i   Susan, b. ——, m. ——, Keniston of Weare, N. H.

419 ii   Samuel, b. ——, ——, drowned.

128 Winthrop[6], b. 17 June, 1789, m. 1st.——,Jemima Headstock of Weare, 2d. —— in Canada, 3d. ——, in Ohio, lived at Vermillion City, Harrison Co., Ohio, and had issue by 1st wife.

420 i   William Clinton, b. in Weare, m. ——, of Boston, Mass., and had two girls.

† 421 ii   Calvin Ira, b. 31 Oct., 1817, m. 16 Feb. 1842, Diantha A. Worden, in Waterville, Me.

422 iii   Sylvia, b. ——, m. ——, Habbard, lives in Wayne, Wayne, Co., Mich.

423 iv   Caroline, b. ——, m. ——, Frazier in E. Weare, N. H.

424 v   425 vi, 426 vii, 427 viii, 428 ix, 429 x, by last wife.

129 Jonathan[6], Served in the war of 1812, was a sea captain until about 45 years of age, then a farmer in Seabrook for a year or so, settled in Salisbury in 1822, now living.

430 i   Margaret L., b. 9 Nov. 1816, m. 22 Jan. 1839, Jos W. Currier, Salisbury.

431 ii   Hannah G. b. 5 Nov., 1820, m. 24 Dec. 1846, Jacob B. Collins, Salisbury, d. 17 Mar., 1847.

432 iii   Abigail E , b. 12 Oct., 1823, unmarried, ——, d. 25 May, 1876.

433 iv   Calesta B., b. 28 Oct., 1825, m. 14 Dec., 1843, Jno. L. Pillsbury, Salisbury, d. 27 June, 1859.

† 434 v   John L., b. 26 Oct., 1827, m. 28 May, 1853, Mary A. Morrill, Salisbury.

† 435 vi   Moses T., b. 25 Jan., 1830, m. 13 Feb. 1849, Sarah A. Eaton.

436 vii   Mary T. b. 25 July, 1834, m. ——, d. 13 Feb., 1835.

132 John[6], b. ——, m, 15 Dec., 1786, Mary Murch, lived in Gorham and Windham, Me.

437 i   Rebecca, b. ——, m. ——, William Riggs, s p. d —— æ. 76.

† 438 ii   David, b. 15 July, 1790, m. 1st. 1814, Lucy Marsh, 2d. 1820, Hannah Lombard, d. ——, æ. 82.

† 439 iii   John, b. 3 Oct., 1792, m. 28 Oct., 1821, Lydia Moulton, d. 21 Dec., 1840, d. 10 Nov. 1875

440 iv   Mary, b. ——, m,—— Samuel Bolton.

441 v   Fanny, b. ——, m —— Joel Libby.

† 442 vi   Ephraim, b. 5 Jan. 1798, m. 22 Mar, 1820, Mathew Bacon, d. 21 May. 1874.

† 443 vii   William, b. 30 Jan., 1800, m. 1st. 1824, Joanna Briggs, 1827, Mary H. Hicks, d. 11 July, 1871, living.

444 viii   Ezra, b. ——, went to sea and was never heard from.

445 ix   Hannah Jordan, b.——, 1804, m. ——, 1st. —— Cook, 2d. ——, Jordan.

133 William⁶, b. ——; m. 1st, 12 May, 1793, Sarah Bonney of Turner, Me; 2nd, Miss Waterhouse. Moved from Buckfield, Me., to Machias. Died 1837. Children by first wife:

446 i   Fanny, b. in Buckfield, 10 Oct., 1795; m. ——, Edward Forster; died in
           Calais, 7 June, 1842.

447 ii   William, b. ——; m. ——, Lydia Everell; d. 19 August, 1853.

† 448 iii   Joseph, b. ——; m. ——, Mary Stickney; d. 15 Dec., 1848.

449 iv   Clark, b. ——; unmarried; drowned at St. Johns, N. B., 10 Sept., 1852.

† 450 v   John, b. ——; m. ——; said to have a son David.

451 vi   Fayetta, b. ——; m. ——, Samuel Smith, and had one child; d. ——.

Children by second wife :

452 vii   Tetter, b. ——; dead.

453 viii   Otis, b. ——; dead.

137 Benjamin⁶, b. in Gorham, Me., 1761, Enlisted in the Revolutionary war when 18 years of age and served three years under Capt. Abner Wade of Col. M. Jackson's regiment. Married, first, 9 April, 1793, Martha Parson; 2d, 22 Sept., 1803, Sally Newt of Buckfield, Me. Was a U. S. pensioner. Died 1842. *1846*

BY FIRST WIFE:

† 454 i   Isaac, b. 16 Aug., 1796, m. —— Sarah Cilley, (470); d. 19 Oct., 1819.

455 ii

456 iii   John, b. 12 April 1798; unmarried; d. — Oct., 1819.

457 iv

† 458 v   William Woodhouse, b. 13 July, 1800; m. 1st, 2 April, 1820, Fanny Runnell;
           2d, 5 March, 1856, Sarah Hawes. Living.

† 459 vi   Samuel, b. 2 June, 1802; m. 1st, Rhoda Phenix; died 14 April, 1835; 2d,
           Hannah Corbett. Living

460 vii   Martha, b. 31 May, 1803; m. Moses Cilley of Knox, (478); d. 24 June,
           1829.

461 viii   Edna, b. —— 1804; m. Morrill Thompson, Vt ; d. ——, 1827.

462 ix   Lucy b. ——, 1805; m. ——, 1821, Ezra Crane. Living

463 x   Susanna, b. 3 Jan. 1806; m. 19 Nov. 1819, Judah Cilley, (479); d 27 Aug.
           1853.

464 xi   Dolly, b. 26 Sept., 1810; m. 5 March, 1830, Mark Scribner; d. 30 April,
           1877. He d. 21 April, 1866.*

---

* Of them their daughter, Mrs. Bridgham, writes: "They moved to Charleston in 1832 and commenced a pioneer life, clearing the land and working with willing hands to establish a comfortable home for themselves and children, meeting with moderate success, as the old homestead testifies, which was a home of comfort while they lived and endeared by many pleasant associations to those left behind. It was my mother's nature to give herself unreservedly for the good of her family and all around her. With limited means, she managed to give her children a fair education, devoting much time to them herself. Small in stature, quiet and unassuming, a true gentlewoman always. She gained the respect and love of all with whom she came in contact. Blessed little mother!" Children:

3

465 xii Fayetta, b. 15 June 1811; m. 19 Oct. 1836, Ezra Hanson. Living
466 xiii Phebe, b. ——, 1812; m. ——, 1837, Simon Cilley, Jr.. (483); d. 29 April, 1835.
† 467 xiv Emerson, b. 24 Jan., 1815; m. Florilla Roberts. Living.
468 xv Sally, b. ——, 1825; m. Jacob Rendell, China, Me. Living.

142 Peter,[6] b. ——, 1768; m. Patty Teague. Moved to Brooks, Me.; a farmer. Died 1856, Æ 87. Children : ·

469 i Nancy, b. 15 April, 1794; m. Luther Fogg of Brooks, Me., d. 6 May, 1854; d. 21 April, 1868.
470 ii Sarah, b. 14 May, 1796; m. 1st, Isaac Cilley, (454); m. 2d, Abner Ham; d. 24 June, 1874.
471 iii Hannah, b. 27 July, 1798; m. John Pilley; d. 10 Dec., 1875
† 472 iv Peter, Jr., b. 11 Nov. 1802; m. Polly Cilley, (480.) Living.
† 473 v Joseph, b. 14 June, 1805; m. 1st, 11 Jan., 1827, Betsey Gilman; m. 2d, 12 April, 1858, Mrs. Lucretia (Achorn) Porter; d. 15 May, 1871.
† 474 vi Benjamin, b. 5 Sept. 1809; m. 1st, 20 Oct. 1831, Mahala Piper; m. 2d, Mary Folsom. Living.
475 vii Martha b. ——, 1819; m. Arthur Hall; d. ——, 1875.

143 Simon,[6] b. ——, 1774; m. Polly Teague of Turner, who d. 15 June, 1859, Æ 84. A house carpenter, Brooks. Served in the war of 1812 under Capt. Gilbreth, in Gen. Brown's command. At the Battle of Bridgewater, (vide Col. Joseph (217) for a description of this battle) Niagara and Chippewa. Died 13 Nov. 1847. Children :

476 i Elizabeth, b 31 Jan., 1797; m. Wm. Bassie; d. 5 July, 1867.
† 477 ii Darling, b. 23 April, 1798; m. Esther Frost; d. 22 Aug., 1875.
† 478 iii Moses, b. 28 April, 1800; m. 1st, Martha Cilley, (460); 2d, Lydia Roberts; d. 8 June, 1834.
† 479 iv Judah, b. 28 Aug., 1801; m. 1st, Nov., 1819, Susannah Cilley, (463) d. 27 Aug , 1853; 2d, Cordelia Frost. Living.
480 v Polly, b. 25 April 1803; m Peter Cilley (472;) d. 29 June, 1869.
481 vi Fanny, b. ——, 1805; m. Caleb Lambert Living.
482 vii Ann, b. 15 Oct., 1810; m. John Mathews. Living.
† 483 viii Simon, Jr., b. 23 Dec. 1811; m. 1st, 1836, Phebe Cilley, (466); 2d, 1852, Hannah Scribner. Living.
484 ix Deborah b. 5 March, 1816; m. James Douglass; d. 10 June, 1871.

---

i Caroline, E. T., b. 9 Nov. 1834; a teacher in Utah. ii Mary J., b. 8 Dec., 1836; m 20 March, 1858, Joseph Bridgham. Have one child, Kate M., b. 2 Feb., 1864. iii Daniel Whitman, b. 8 Dec., 1838; m. 18 March, 1874, Sarah H. Stevens A stock broker at Salt Lake City. iv Newell, b. 30 April, 1842. Lives in Utah; raises horses. v Alvenia F., b. 16 May, 1844; m. 11 May 1873, John M. Carey, druggist at Bad Axe, Mich. Have Ursula, b. 11 Oct., 1875, and Charles C., b. 23 Feb., 1877. vi Charles H., b. 28 August 1849. Harness maker, Michigan.

144 Daniel⁶, b. 1 March, 1762, m. ——, 1784, Anna Ellsworth, b. 5 Aug., 1758, and d. 27 Feb., 1829; d. in Tunbridge, Vt., 13 Nov., 1838.

† 485 i   David, b. 5 June, 1785, m. 1 Jan. 1809, Abigail Church; d. 6 Mar., 1861.

486 ii   Judith, b. 3 Feb., 1787; unmarried, d. in Tunbridge, Vt., 19 Apr., 1820.

487 iii   Otis, b. 27 July, 1789; unmarried, d. 22 Nov., 1819.

† 488 iv   Josiah, b. 16 Feb , 1791, m. 7 Mar , 1816, Susan Tucker; d. 7 June, 1858.

† 489 'v   John, b. 6 July, 1793, m. 13 Mar., 1817, Sally Tucker; d. 2 Feb , 1873.

490 vi   Abagail, b. 27 Aug., 1795; d. 20 March, 1799.

491 vii   Polly, b 17 Dec., 1798, m. 23 Oct., 1839, Abijah Powers; living in Hanover, N. H.

† 492 viii   Eben, b 4 March, 1800, m. Aug., 1824, Sabina Leeds; living Patuxet, R I.

† 493 ix   Moses, b. 5 Sept , 1803, m. April, 1842, Lydia Richardson; d. 16, Feb., 1858, in Shelford.

146 Benjamin⁶ (called Great Ben), b. 14 Oct., 1765, m. 29 Oct., 1788, Sarah Wadleigh of Andover.

† 494 i   Calvin, b. ——, m ——.

† 495 ii   Greenleaf, b ——, m. ——.

† 496 iii   Thomas Jefferson, m. Sally Proctor.

497 iv   Sophy, b. ——, m. 11 June, 1818, Josiah Sanborn.

147 Ebenezer⁶, b. 22 Nov., 1767, in Rye (?) N. H. When about 25 years of age, came to Vermont, and married Polly, dau. of William and Molly, or Polly, (Hoyt) Clement, of Tunbridge, Vt.

498 i   Abagail, b. 24 April, 1794, m. 1 March, 1815, Otis Hoyt; d. 1855. Had Henry C., Andrew J., Martha C., Marshall, Rollin C. M. Don Carlos m. Eliza A. Eaton. and Jennett. Charles B. F. m. Caroline P. Atwood.

† 499 ii   Jasper, b. 13 May, 1796, m. ——.

500 iii   Matilda, b. 10 July, 1798, m. 2 Dec., 1819, Rufus Hoyt; d. 20 July, 1850. Had Jason B., Mary F., and Charlotte M

† 501 iv   Mayhew b 1 July, 1800, m 2 Aug., 1823, Margarette Dolbar of Candia, N.H.; d. 17 Feb., 1830.

502 v   Ruby, b. 16 July, 1802, m. 23 Mar. 1828, Henry Douglass; d. 8 Mar., 1868.

503 vi   Washington, b. 12 Jan., 1805, m. Mrs Tansy M Peckham, no issue; d. in New York City, 1 Jan., 1858.

504 vii   Betsy, b. 4 July, 1807, m. 10 Mar. 1828, E. C. Abbott

505 viii   John, b. 28 July, 1809, m. 1833, Martha H. Moring. Lives in Jersey city; no issue.

506 ix   Clement, b. 20 Dec., 1811; d. 15 Feb., 1813.

* 507 x   Wealthy, b. 9 March 1814, m 12 Oct., 1837, Allen S. Vail.

---

* Wealthy and Allen S. Vail reside in Worcester, Vt., and have: i Agnes Gertrude, b. 24 July, 1838, m. 14 April, 1870, Elijah Whitney of Middlesex, a farmer. ii Emma Eugenia, b. 30 July, 1840; d 26 Feb , 1847. iii Martha Ann, b 17 Sept., 1841, m. 25 Dec. 1867, Geo. W. Dunham of Northfield, resides in Worcester, Vt., a farmer. iv Henry Douglass, b. 13 June, 1843, m. 1 Jan., 1875, Abbie Ann Templeton—is a merchant, resides in Worcester, Vt. v Washington Eldridge, b. 25 Dec., 1849, m. 25 Dec., 1874, Irun C. Bancroft of Calais, Vt ; is a salesman, resides in Montpelier, Vt.

508 xi Orris Peabody, b. 23 Sept., 1816, m. 4 March, 1846, Caroline, dau. of David
and Sally (Hoyt) Jones; no issue.

* 509 xii Louisa, b. 23 March, 1819, m. 20 April, 1840, Rev. W. B. Howard.

148 William[6], b. in N. H., m. Abagail, b. 26 July 1774, dau.
of Hon. William and Lucy (Church) Ward. Resided at Poultney
and Underhill, and lastly at Jericho, Vt., where he d. 6 April,
1847.

510 i Lindamira, b. 6 May, 1797; m. 20 Nov., 1825, Marshall Castle, and had
Hawley, b. 4 Aug., 1827; d. 5 April, 1875.

511 ii Lucy, b. 5 June, 1799; m. 3 Dec , 1818, Almon Fennell; d. 9 April, 1813,
and had William G., b , 7 June, 1823; unm. Rollin C., b. 25 Feb.,
1825; d at Jericho, 13 Aug., 1855.

† 512 iii William Ward, b. 20 Sept., 1801; m. Feb., 1830, Roxanna Castle.

† 513 iv Spencer, b. 12 June, 1804; m. 25 Sept , 1823, Atara Ward; d. 20 March,
1859.

514 v Eliza,‡ b. 30 Nov. 1806; m. 1 Dec., 1831, Pearl Castle.

515 vi Albert, b. 24 Sept., 1809; m. 1st, 1 Dec., 1831, Abagail Castle; d. 22 Oct.,
1873; 2d, 4 July, 1875, Ednah J. Foster; 3 p.

516 vii Emily,§ b. 17 May, 1812; m. 18 April 1841, Ira Abbey of Essex, Vt.

† 517 viii Andrew Jackson, b. 30 June, 1814; m. 11 Sept., 1841, Lucretia Hill.

150 Jacob,[6] b. ——, 1774 ; m. 1st, 7 Jan., 1799, Sally Chase
of Salisbury, who d. ——, 1804; 2d, 1805, Sally Cheney; d. 15
May, 1847; d. 13 Oct., 1534. By first wife :

518 i Martha R., b. ——, 1802; m. ——, 1823, Dav. Chase Hall; d. 1876.

519 ii Roxanie C., b. ——, 1804; m. ——. 1830, Joseph Straw.

By second wife :

520 iii Sally Chase, b. 9 Sept., 1806; m. 30 Dec., 1830, Simon Sanborn.

521 iv Mary L , b. 13 Sept , 1808· m. 24 Nov., 1834, Amand Osman; d. 27 Feb.,
1871.

522 v ‖Abagail Clark, b. 13 Dec., 1809; m. 3 Feb., 1836, Amos R. Hood.

---

* Lonisa and the Rev. W. B. Howard reside in Highgate Center, Vt , and have:
i William Clement, b. 14 April, 1841, in Montpelier, Vt., m. in Wardsboro, Vt , 11 Jan.
1872, Sereeta A. (Fitts) Burnham; resides in Aurora, Ill. ii Helen Louise, b. 29 July,
1845, in Lowell, Mass , m in Alburgh, Vt., 23 July, 1871, Rev. Martin E. Cady of
Middlebury, Vt., late Principal of the Troy Conf. Academy, and present Principal of
Rock River Conf. Seminary, Aurora, Ill. iii Walter Eugene, b. 29 May, 1849, in Tunbridge, Vt ; entered Middleburg College in 1867, and graduated in 1871; is Principal
of the State Normal School, Castleton, Vt.

‡ Eliza and Pearl Castle res. Essex, Vt., and had Herman F., b. 23 May, 1839; d. 6
Sept., 1844, Mary E , b. 23 June, 1846.

§ Had issue, Pearl Castle, b. 6 Feb., 1842; m. 4 March, 1863, Martha Ermina Weed
of Essex, Vt.

‖ Children of Abagail C. and Amos R. Hood: Wm. Francis, b. 3 Jan., 1837; m. 20
Nov., 1866, Maria L. Burgess. Julia Augusta, b. 21 June, 1839; m. 8 Feb., 1863, J.
G. Rogers. Charles J., b. 11 Dec., 1845, and Arcelia C., b. 17 Oct., 1847.

523 vi   Benjamin, b. 1 Jan.. 1811; d. 11 Sept., 1811.
524 vii Emmiline, b., ———, 1812; d. 1 Jan., 1813.
525 viii Julia Abbott, b. 14 June, 1814; d. 20 June, 1830.
† 526 ix Wm. Laurentine, b 9 Sept , 1817; m. 25 April, 1839, Lucy C. Sanborn.
527 x   Augusta Marcia, b. 14 Feb., 1822; m. 7 Oct , 1840, Daniel C. Eaton.
528 xi Jacob Francis, b. 22 Feb., 1830. Lives in Chicago.

153 Satchel[6], settled in Mendon, Munroe Co., N. Y. Was a contractor for public works; m. 16 Feb., 1809, Wealthy, dau. of Jedediah and Olive (Whipple) Cummings, who d. 20 June, 1853.

† 529 i   John J , b. 7 May, 1810; m. 1 July, 1832, Mandana Lamkin; d. 4 March, 1861.
530 ii Erasmus A., b. 18 March, 1812; d. 2 May, 1813.
531 iii Mary Ann, b. 6 May, 1814; m. 1st, 1 August, 1831, Orlando Putnam; 2d, 22 Feb., 1835, S. D. Couloyne, Lisbon, Noble Co , Ind.
532 iv Olive A , b. 26 Feb., 1816; m. 26 Feb. 1833, Elijah Southard; d. 28 May, 1837.
533 v   Augusta B , b. 26 April, 1819; d. 4 May, 1820.
534 vi Ezra M., b. 5 April, 1821; d. 28 March, 1823.
† 535 vii Jacob S., b. 21 July, 1823; m. 14 March, 1844, Mary A. Seaman.
536 viii Wealthy S , b. 23 Feb., 1826; m. 1st, 4 Jan., 1844, Joseph Guber; 2d, ——— Hill, Petersburgh, Mich.
537 ix James W., b. 23 June, 1828. Served under Gen. Zach. Taylor during the Mexican War, after which went to Ohio, and has not been heard from for 26 years.
538 x   Emily, b. 10 Sept., 1830; m. 19 Dec., 1847, Calvin Lamkin; d. Hamlin, Munroe Co , Michigan.

155 Clark,[6] m. ———. Resided in Livonia, Livingston, Co., N. Y., in 1861, and had 4 children there.

539 i Erasmus, b. ———; 540 ii Hannah, b. ———; 541 iii Harriet, b. ———; 542 iv ——, b. ———; 543 v —— ; 544 vi ——.

156 Elisha[6] (Celley), m. Sarah Keniston, who was b. 13 Dec. 1768; d. 12 Nov., 1851. Was a farmer. Lived in Corinth, Vt.

545 i   Sarah, b. 14 Feb., 1787; d. 11 Aug , 1788.
† 546 ii Joel, b. 7 July, 1789, m. 17 May, 1811, Phebe Blanchard of Woodbury, Vt.; d. 19 July, 1849.
547 iii Sarah, b. 24 Dec., 1791; d. 24 Feb , 1793.
† 548 iv Elisha, b. 21 June, 1794, m. 30 April, 1833, Priscilla Banfill, and had Erastus, b. 18 June, 1837; d. 23 Sept., 1838. He was Captain of a cavalry company in the war of 1812, and a farmer.
† 549 v Benjamin, b. 8 Aug., 1796, m. 1st, 7 March, 1830, Nancy Kingsbury; 2d, 5 March, 1837, Jane Sawyer; 3d, 5 Sept., 1845, Ann Sawyer; 4th, 20 March, 1855, Harriet Sawyer.

† 550 vi William, b. 7 Oct , 1798, m. 1st, 14 Oct., 1818, Fannie Norcross; 2d, 26 July 1865, Hannah Smith.

551 vii Susanna, b. 11 Jan., 1801; d 14 Sept , 1843.

† 552 viii John, b. 24 Sept., 1803, m. 15 Dec., 1836, Lavinia Greenleaf; has one dau. Lives in Corinth, Vt.

* 553 ix Apphia, b. 15 June, 1806, m. 1st, 13 Feb., 1835, Gregory Durgin of Andover, N. H.; 2d, 28 June, 1861, Israel C. Willard.

554 x Sarah, b. 14 Feb., 1809; d. 29 Sept., 1811

555 xi Polly, b. 7 Oct., 1813, m. Jan , 1839, Michar Norcross of Bradford, Vt ; d. 29 June, 1853. Had issue: John G , b. 17 Oct., 1840, m. 4 Dec , 1864, Lizzie A. Rowe; Alvin C., b. 19 Dec., 1842, m. 22 Dec., 1865, Maria Taylor; Susan E., b. 8 Jan , 1845, d. 18 Mar., 1868; Ellis W., b. 17 July, 1849, m. 24 Aug., 1872, Celia E. Eastman.

157 Benjamin,[6] (lived at Mompey Hill); m. Judith, (171) dau. of Aaron Cilley (59). Moved to Orange, Vt.

† 556 i Ai, b. ——; m. Betsey Shepherd. Moved to Orange, Vt.

557 ii Benjamin, b. ——; m. —— Clifford. No issue.

† 558 iii Aaron, b. ——; Hannah Clifford, sister to above. Went to Vt.

559 iv Jabish, b. ——; unmarried; d. ——.

560 v Hiram, b. ——. Went to Vt.

561 vi Betsey, b. 7 April, 1795; m. 4 July, 1820, Eben Currier, brother of E. C. Cilley's (637) mother; d. 15 June, 1863. Had George, b , 1818. John, b. Dec., 1820; d. April, 1825. Lydia, b. Sept., 1822; d. 15 April, 1837. John T. M., b. July, 1824. Benjamin, b. 26 July, 1826. Ebenezer, b. 5 July, 1828. Albert E., b. 31 July, 1830; Charles E., b , 7 Sept., 1832. James, b. 6 Feb., 1835. Stephen C., b. 1 March, 1838; d. 4 Juyl, 1860. Abigail M., b. 7 May, 1840.

562 vii Priscilla, b. ——; m —— Marshall.

563 viii Judith, b. ——; unmarried.

158 Philip,[6] b. in Poplin ; m. Priscilla Keniston, dau. of ——. A Farmer. Died 5 Nov., 1816.

564 i Affie, b. 8 Nov., 1791; m. 30 May, 1813, Charles Keniston.

† 565 ii Francis, b. 24 Nov., 1793; m. 5 March, 1818, Judith Scribner. Served in the war of 1812.

‡ 566 iii Sally, b. 22 Oct., 1795; m. 1st, 14 July, 1833, Joshua Seavey; d. 20 July, 1849; 2d, 17 Nov , 1853, Stephen Brown; d. 11 Aug , 1864. Living.

---

*Gregory and Apphia had: Daniel C., b. 23 July, 1837; Elisha C., b. 8 July, 1838, m. 9 July, 1872, Alice M. Curtis; Alvin M., b. 15 March, 1840, m. 1 Jan , 1865, Louise C. Berry; Joseph W., b. 12 March, 1842, d. 2 July, 1844; Martha, b. 15 July, 1844, d. 16 July, 1850; Allen J., b. 12 March, 1846, d. 24 April, 1869; Gregory B., b. 8 March, 1848, m. 7 April, 1873, Sarah E Ormsby, d. 20 Deo , 1876.

‡Sally and Joshua Seavey had: 1, Susan b. 14 July, 1834; m. 6 Aug., 1853, Jesse F. Wilson; 2, Eleanora F., b. 19 May, 1836; m. 4 July, 1853, Jacob B. Moar; d. 18 Oct , 1864. Plunia F., b. 19 March, 1838; d. 8 Oct., 1839.

567 iv   Mariam, b. 6 Nov., 1797; m. April, 1820, Isaac Downes, who was b. in
Lebanon, Mo., 1790, and d March 15, 1848, in Andover. Issue:
1. Philip C., b. 19 Oct., 1821; d. 26 Sept , 1863, s. p. 2. Leonard W.,
b. 18 July, 1823; m. Sarah Hill of Thornton, N. H ; d. 8 June, 1857;
3. Phebe A., b. 1825; d. 1833. 4. Priscilla, b 22 Feb., 1828; m.
1850, Eben H. Wilkinson of Effingham, N. H 5. Lydia C , b. 18
Feb , 1830; m. 15 July, 1848, Mark Jesse Leavenworth of Wheelock,
Vt., and had Byron Malines, b. 5 Aug., 1849 Stella Maria, b. 17
Aug., 1852; d 16 July, 1853. Mark Henry, b 9 Feb., 1860; d 4
April, 1862. 6. Ann, b 31 May, 1833; m. 1st, 1852, Charles Warren
of Charleston, Vt.; 2d, 1861, Albert C. Currier. 7. Daniel b. 10
June, 1835; m. 3 July, 1856, Nancy Jane Keniston. 8. Ellen M , b.
6, May, 1837; m. Sept., 1853, Eben Wilkinson; d. 9 Feb., 1856. 9.
Isaac, b 22 April, 1841; m. May, 1867, Abbie A. Sleeper of Andover,
N. H.

† 568 v   Moses, b. 18 Feb , 1800; m Lydia Dunham.

† 569 vi   Jonathan, b Oct., 1801; m. 13 Oct , 1830, Deborah Hill; d April, 1876.

† 570 vii   Benjamin Darling, b. May, 1803; m. 23 Sept , 1837, Priscilla Keniston;
d. March —, 1876.

570.1 viii   William b. 1804; d. 1826.

† 571 ix   Phillip, b , March, 1808; m. 1 Sept., 1834, Sarah Cole; d. March, 1861.

† 572 x   David K , b. 9 May, 1813; m. 21 Nov., 1836, Polly Keniston; d. 9 Aug.,
1874.

† 573 xi   John, b., 22 Aug , 1815; m. Mary M. M. Carter. Resides in East Dixfield,
Me.

160   Job⁶, b. in Poplin, N. H., m. Susan, dau. of George and
Hannah (Flood) Seava of Deerfield, N. H. A farmer in Hebron,
N. H.

574 i   Lydia D , b 26 March, 1799; unmarried, d. 8 Aug., 1877.

575 ii   Rebecca, b. 31 Aug., 1800, m Ezra G. Tuft, Cambridge, Mass.

576 iii   Job, b. 26 Feb., 1802; d. 1856.

577 iv   Hannah, b. 16 Dec., 1803; m. Russel Wright of Haverhill, N. H.

578 v   Henry, b. 25 April, 1806, m. 1845, Abbie Johnson, Ellsworth; d. 3 Dec., 1870.

† 579 vi   Andrew, b. 15 March, 1808; m. 26 Sept , 1830, Charlotte Leeds, Charlestown,
Mass.

580 vii   Eunice B., b. 20 Feb., 1810; m. 20 Dec., 1831, Thomas Stearns. Paris, Me.

581 viii   Roxana, b. 1812.

† 582 ix   George W., b. 14 Aug., 1814; m. 19 Feb., 1844, Laura A. Steward.

583 x   Nathaniel, b. 1816.

584 xi   Jonathan, b. 1818.

585 xii   Sarah, b. 1820.   586 xiii ——.

161   Stephen⁶, m. Abagail, dau. of Ebenezer and Lydia Bean
Currier; a farmer in Andover, N. H.

587 i   Lydia, b. 30 Nov., 1807; d. 28 Nov., 1843.

588 ii   Cynthia, b. 27 Dec., 1809; m. 5 April, 1832, Jeremiah Roberts. Living in.
Andover, Ct.

162 William[6], m. 1st, ——, 2d, ——.

BY FIRST WIFE.

589 i Mary, b. 1802.

590 ii John B., b. 15 Feb., 1810, m.——; d. in Fairfax, Vt.

BY SECOND WIFE.

591 iii ——. 592 iv ——. 593 v ——.

163 Elijah[6], m. Rhoda, dau. of Volentine and Comfort Keniston. A farmer and cordwainer, Andover, N. H.

† 594 i Isaac, b. 4 May, 1804; m Nov., 1835, Susan Gilman.

595 ii Nancy, b 3 Dec., 1806; m. 17 Dec , 1837, Samuel Elkins. Lives in Potter Place, Andover, N. H., and had: Frank P., b. 16 Dec., 1849, m. 26 Nov. 1866; Joseph W , b. 8 Dec., 1840; Jeremiah S., b. 8 Jan., 1842, m. 16 March, 1869; Lucinda P., b. 16 March, 1844, m. 11 Aug , 1871, d. 19 Aug., 1872; Marcia A., b. 19 Dec., 1846, m. 15 Oct., 1871; Scott W. S., b. 2 Feb., 1848, d. 27 June, 1851; Sarah E., b. 9 April, 1850, d. 2 April, 1851.

† 596 iii John, b. 15 Aug., 1808; m. 15 Aug., 1828, Sarah Bruce.

597 iv Rebecca, b. 9 Sept., 1810, m. 1836, Wm. Davies, s. p.; d.——.

598 v Sarah, b 1813; d. 1817.

599 vi Lucinda, b. 1815, m. 1837, Alen F. Pool; res. Cranston, R. I , s. p.

168 Joseph[6], b. 4 Aug., 1778, in Salisbury, N. H.; m. 20 June, 1803, Susan, dau. of Henry and Hannah (Straw) Springer, who was b. in Canaan, N. H., 7 Mar., 1784, d. 7 Aug., 1866. A farmer in Andover, N. H.; d. 2 May, 1827.

600 i Betsy S., b. 20 Sept., 1804, m. 3 Mar., 1831, Sanders Herbert of Franklin, N. H., and had Susan, Judith, and two boys; d. 7 Aug., 1866.

601 ii Nancy M., b. 19 Aug., 1806; m. 24 May, 1838, Asa Morrison of Hopkinton, N. H. Resides in Michigan.

602 iii Sarah C., b. 13 July, 1810, m. 4 Sept., 1828, Enoch George of Ackworth, N. H., and had Joseph C., Alonzo N., Melissa, Morrison, Lucinda, and Henry. She d. May 20, 1868.

603 iv Lucinda, b. 25 Sept., 1812; d. 3 Sept., 1837.

604 v Hannah S., b. 11 Aug., 1814; m. 6 Oct , 1833, Samuel Hoyt of Bradford, N. H. and had: Joseph C , Benj F., Susan A., Nettie, Caroline R., and Clarinda. She d. Jan. 1, 1864.

605 vi Abagail C., b. 26 Feb., 1816; m. 19 Jan., 1837, Asa S. Muzzey of Lowell, Mass., and had George A. and S. Eugene.

† 606 vii Samuel C., b. 13 May, 1819, m. 3 July, 1841, Caroline Bickford; d 20th Nov., 1856.

607 viii Relief S , b. 12 Aug., 1823, m. 26 Dec , 1848, William Trow, Jr , of Sunapee, N. H., and had: George C., b. 7 Dec., 1849; Abbie L , b. 24 July, 1851, m. 29 Nov., 1877, Paige A Boynton of Weare, N. H.; Eugene F., b. 14 April, 1853, d. 16 Dec., 1857; Charles H., b 1 Jan., 1856, d. 14 April, 1857; Alice V., b 2 June, 1858; Willie S., b. 11 Feb , 1860; Charles A., b. 31 Mar., 1862; Joseph H., b. 30 May, 1865; Atherton U., b. 16 April, 1867.

170 Samuel[6], b. 30 Oct., 1791; m. 1st, 30 April, 1812, Mary Blaisdell, b. 10 Nov., 1792, d. 22 Sept., 1812; m. 2d, 10 Feb., 1823, Hannah P. Parker, b. 30 April, 1709, d. 3 July, 1849; m. 3d, 30 Oct., 1849, Ann Avery, b. 10 July, 1805. A farmer. Died 3 Jan., 1876.

BY FIRST WIFE.

608 i   Hannah, b. 16 July, 1812, d 16 Mar , 1813.

609 ii   Hannah, b. 7 Dec., 1813, m. ——, Joseph Philbrick, and had a son, d. 12 Aug., 1844.

610 iii   Mary, b. 18 Dec., 1815, m. ——, Lowell Brown, and had Mary, Charles and Cora, d. 10 Nov., 1854.

611 iv   Charles, b. 28 June, 1819, d. 11 April, 1821.

612 v   Harriet B., b. 26 June, 1821, m. 1st, 12 Dec., 1837, Chase Osgood, and had Eveline F., b. 16 Dec., 1838, Fred'k F., b. 23 Dec., 1842 : m. 2d, 20 June, 1848, George W. Sargent, and had Nancy E., b. 10 Feb., 1849, d. 1 Feb., 1871, Amanda H , b. 9 Feb., 1855, George H., b. 23 May, 1856, Sam. Eddy, b. 1 March, 1862, d. 13 Dec , 1864.

BY THIRD WIFE

613 vi   Hannah A., b. 7 Aug., 1850, d. 17 Feb., 1862.

171 Charles,[6] b. 9 Feb., 1795; m. 16 Oct., 1820, Betsey Mowe. Served in the war of 1812. Died 27 June, 1827.

614 i   Jane M., b. 2 Aug., 1822, m. 21 Oct., 1845, Eben W. Mason, and had Geo. Carroll, b. 16 Sept , 1847, d 4 Nov., 1875.

†615 ii   John M., b 29 Feb., 1824, m. 7 Nov , 1861, Susan C. Herbert, d. 10 Aug., 1865.

†616 iii   Charles M., b. 13 Feb., 1826, m. 27, May, 1854, Susan E. Stevens.

176 Benjamin[6], b. ——, 1773; m. Sarah Uren; d. 1 May, 1846, æ 67. Resided in Andover; a farmer; d. 3 March, 1812.

617 i   Sally, b. ——, 1800; m. Jona Merey; d. ——.

† 618 ii   Moses T., b. ——, 1802; m. Drusilla Woodward, New London, N. H.; d. 2 June, 1838.

† 619 iii   Aaron, b. 6 May, 1804; m. 1st, 25 Nov., 1826, Sally Carr; 2d, 10 Nov., 1844, Susan Howard.

620 iv   John M., b. ——, 1807; m. ——; d. in Louisville, Ky., 1835.

621 v   Mary, b. ——, 1809; d. 24 Dec., 1816.

622 vi   James W., b. 2 May, 1811; d. in Mechanicsburg, Ohio, 1839.

623 vii   Mehitable, b. ——, 1812; m. 27 Nov., 1833, Col. Jos. B. Carr.

177 Edmund H[6]., b. ——, 1774; m. 11 May, 1802, Mehitable Uren, d. 3 Nov., 1852; d. 18 August, 1834.

624 i   Sally, b. 11 Sept., 1803; d. 31 May, 1828.

625 ii   James, b. 28 Feb., 1806; m. 1st, Betsey Carr of Wilmot; 2d, 9 July, 1837, Theodate Rowe.

626 iii   Reuben, b. 17 April, 1808; d 6 April, 1815.

627 iv   Edmund, b. 19 June, 1811; d. 20 Nov., 1816.

628 v Benjamin, b. 25 June, 1813; m. 1st, 31 Dec., 1835, Sally Brown; d. 9 Jan., 1842; 2d, 7 Oct. 1845, Mary Brown, sister to above; d. 18 Sept., 1863.

629 vi Reuben, 2d., b. 22 April, 1816; d 31 Oct , 1820.

630 vii Joel, b. 9 June, 1819; m. 30 July, 1840, Elizabeth Cilley. Went to Maryland when young. Res. Baltimore, s. p.

631 viii Silas M., b. 14 March, 1822, unmarried; d. 7 Oct., 1843.

182 Aaron[6], m. 1st, 8 Nov., 1803, Meriam Sleeper, 2d, 30 Jan., 1806, Lydia Currier, b. 12 Aug., 1787, d. 27 June, 1858. He lived in Andover; was a farmer, Justice of the Peace, a select-man for several years, member of the Legislature for two years, and a prominent Freemason.

† 632 i Aaron, b. 3 Feb , 1807, m. 1st, 29 Dec., 1825, Eliza Rolfe, 2d, 8 Sept , 1839, Emily Severns; d. 22 July, 1870.

633 ii Miriam, b. 2 Oct., 1808, m. 13 Nov., 1827, Sam'l Morrill; d. 11 May, 1842.

† 634 iii John B., b. 10 Sept , 1810, m. 26 Oct., 1835, Mercy A. Taylor of Harvard, Mass., d. 24 May, 1870.

† 635 iv Benjamin D., b. 10 Oct , 1812, m. 1st, 1 Jan , 1847, Sarah A. Dalton, 2d, 28 Oct , 1860, Emma J. Severns; d. 8 Dec., 1876.

636 v Lydia, b. 28 Jan , 1815; d. 15 April, 1825.

† 637 vi Ebenezer C., b. 6 April, 1816, m. 4 June, 1846, Phebe A. Cilley.

† 638 vii Andrew J , b. 16 July, 1818, m. 1st, 20 March, 1842, Nancy J. Severns, 2d, May, 1846, Susan Bowman, 3d, 3 July, 1853, Mrs. Susan (Bartlett) Marshall.

639 viii Abagail, b 18 July, 1820, m, 5 May, 1842, John Bailey.

640 ix Adaline, b. 2 Sept., 1823; d. 26 March, 1835.

641 x William W., b. 27 Dec , 1830, m. —— Lives in Colorado.

183 Jabez[6], b. ——, 1786; m. 1st, Miss Dolly Gove of Wilmot; 2d, 30 July, 1817, Mehitable, b. 27 April, 1790, sister of Lydia and dau. of Ebenezer Currier, a soldier of the revolution. Child by 1st wife :

† 642 i Nathan G., b. 29 Aug , 1811; m. 21 Nov , 1834, Amy S. Phelps.

Children by 2d wife :

643 ii Jasper H., b. 15 August, 1813; m Mary Rowell. Lives in Franklin, N. H., s. p.

† 644 iii Asa B., b. 23 Dec., 1817; m. Harriet Sanborn.

† 645 iv Stephen F., b. 13 June, 1820; m. 26 May, 1841, Mary A. Mitchell.

646 v William H., b. 21 Sept , 1822. Blacksmith, Modesta, Cal.

647 vi Mary A., b. ——; m. Solomon Kenniston.

187 George[7], (Silley) m. 1st, Mary A. dau. of John R. and Jane Graffam ; 2d, Sarah E. Holmes, a widow and dau. of John and Betsey Littlefield of Kennebunk, Me. Is a house carpenter and farmer. Enlisted at Augusta, 19 Jan., 1862, in Co. H, 14th Me. Infantry. Served under Gen. Butler until after the battle of

Baton Rouge, then served afterwards under Gen. Banks. Was taken prisoner at St. John's parish, La., and paroled. Discharged for disability, 10 Aug., 1864. Lives in Saco, Me.

648 i   George W., b. 8 Aug., 1860, d. 26 July, 1861.
649 ii   Charles W., b. 16 Sept., 1862, d. 4 Oct., 1864.
650 iii Laura E., b. 13 Feb., 1865.
651 iv Elizabeth A., b. 6 April, 1867.
652 v   Martha T., b. 14 Sept, 1869.

188 Willis,[7] (Cilley) m. Elphronia, b. 26 Feb., 1838, dau. of Aaron and Nancy Batchelder. Lives in South Killingly, Conn.

653 i   Ella E., b. 13 June, 1860.
654 ii   George O., b, 19 Dec., 1861.
655 iii Cora B., b. 20 Jan., 1864.
656 iv Ida D., b. 13 April, 1866.
657 v   Maria E., b. 26 Aug., 1870.
658 vi Charles A., b 25 June, 1872, d 18 July, 1873.
659 vii Esther G., b. 25 April, 1875.

1555841

196 Nathan[7] (Sellea), b. in Saco, Me. Moved to North Yarmouth, m. 1817, Abagail, dau. of William and Elizabeth (Brestow) Wormell, who d. 18 April, 1836. Went to Thomaston in 1819. Was a potter; d. 4 Oct., 1821.

660 i   Mary Ann, b. 28 Feb., 1818; unmarried. Lives in Thomaston.
661 ii   Lucy Phillips, b 22 Nov., 1819, m. 1 Oct., 1837, Henry H. J. Watts, who d. 6 Sept., 1874, and had: 1, Calvin Newton, b. 23 Mar., 1839; 2, Oscar, b. 16 April, 1841; he sailed from San Francisco with Capt Robert Snow in 1866, and the vessel was never heard from; 3, Lucy J., b 24 Aug., 1846; 4, Abagail S., b 9 Jan., 1848; 5, Orris L., b. 19 May, 1849; 6, Leander M., b. 11 May, 1850; 7, Joseph Henry, b. 11 Jan., 1853, d. 27 Sept., 1853.
662 iii Abagail E., b. 10 April, 1821, m. 1st, 1 Sept., 1836, Noah Miller, who d. 16 April, 1845; they had: 1, Nathan S., b. 16 Oct., 1839, d. 9 April, 1875; 2, Edward F., b. 21 May, 1841; m 2d, 1 Nov., 1845, Geo. G. Mitchell, who d. 11 July, 1862; they had Margaret E, b. 8 June, 1846, Lucy, A., b. 3 May, 1848, William F., b. 30 July, 1852, George Benjamin, b. 29 May, 1855, d. 31 Aug., 1855, George G., b. 18 July, 1858.

198 Caleb[7] (Sellea), b. in Saco, m. Elizabeth D. Berry of Limington; d. 18 May, 1825.

† 663 i   Charles H., b. 27 Feb., 1819, m. 1st, Elizabeth Taylor of Wells; 2d, 12 Dec., 1851, Helen Marshall.
664 ii   Mary Ann, b. 16 Oct., 1822, m. 15 Feb., 1843, Jos. Fountain of Saco.

199 Barnard[7] (Sellea), b. in Saco, m. Statira Burnham, b. 12 July, 1798; d. 4 Dec., 1832.

665 i   Charles Henry, b. 2 July, 1825, m. ——, s. p.   Resides in Boston.
† 666 ii   Barnard Gurney, b. 25 June, 1827; married.   Children in Boston.
667 iii   Isabella, b 31 Dec., 1830; died young.

200   Joseph,[7] (Sellea) b. in Saco ; m. 1st, Martha Ann Gordon, who d. 25 January 1833 ; 2d, Mary Jane Johnson ; 3d, July, Melissa Hoyt, who d. July, 1865. Is a farmer and resides in Saco, Me. By 1st wife :

668 i   Sarah Elizabeth, b. 4 July, 1828; m. 27 May, 1855, Harrison D. Harmon, Hiram, Me.
669 ii   Lucy Ann, b. ——; d. young.
670 iii   John, b. ——; d. 19 July, 1833.

By 2d wife :

† 671 iv   William Raight, b 11 Oct., 1835, m. 1 April, 1861.
672 v   Martha A , b. 13 Nov., 1837; m. 13 Oct., 1870, John Lank, Needham, Mass.
673 vi   Joseph, Jr., b. 15 April, 1840. Resides in Ossipee, N. H.

By 3d wife :

674 vii   Lucy, b. 3 April, 1856. Resides in Buxton, Me.
675 viii   Charles E., b. 10 May, 1862. Resides in Hiram, Me.
676 ix   Rufus, b. July, 1863. Resides in Sanford, Me.

202   Oliver[7] (Sellea), b. in Saco.
677 i   Sally, b. ——, 1826.
678 ii   Mary, b. ——.

203   Osman[7] (Sellea), b. in Saco.
679 i   Oliver, b. 18 July, 1832, m. 6 Oct , 1854, Elvesa Half. Was a soldier in Co. H, 5th Me., from Gorham.
680 ii   John, b. 4 March, 1835. Was a soldier in Co. L, 5th Me., from Saco.

207   Benjamin[7] (Cilley), b. in Nottingham. Moved to Ohio with his father ; married. A farmer.
681 i   Selina Dorcas, b. 4 Feb , 1825, m 18 June, 1840.
682 ii   Elizabeth M., b. 19 June, 1826, m. 2 July, 1851, Uriah Rice.
683 iii   Joseph, b. 23 Jan., 1831, m. 1st, 27 Sept., 1853, Mary Hughes, 2d, 24 Dec , 1862, Mary H. Hunt.
684 iv   Martha Ann, b. 28 May, 1832, m. 8 Sept , 1853, James M. Rifner.
685 v   Cecilia, b. 2 July, 1838, m. 10 Nov., 1857, Sam Kessinger Anderson; d. 30 May, 1865.

208   Jonathan[7], b. 7 Jan., 1793, m. 24 Oct., 1830, Sarah, dau. of Rensalaer and Sarah (Heisted) Lee of Saratoga Co., N. Y. Moved West with his father in 1804, and engaged in agricultural pursuits until 21 years of age. Studied law. Took an active part in politics, and was an ardent Jackson Democrat. Was a State Senator in Ohio, an Elector for President Martin Van Buren, and Judge of the Hamilton County Court of Common Pleas in Cincinnati; retired in 1840, and in 1855 removed to Glendale, O. He was an indulgent father, "of high moral character, smooth culture, one of the old school gentlemen." He d. 29 Dec., 1874.

686 i   Josephine Maria, b. 10 April, 1832, m. 6 May, 1852, John Rudolph Neff, Jr., of Philadelphia, and had issue: 1, Randolph Lee, b. 13 Aug., 1853; 2d, Narcissa, b. 8 Dec , 1856; 3d, Sarah Josephine, b. 16 Oct., 1861; 4th, Jonathan Cilley, b. 22 Aug., 1866.

† 687 ii   Rensaleer Lee, b 27 March, 1834, m. 25 April, 1860, Sarah Stanford.

† 688 iii   Henry, b. 16 April, 1836; married.

† 689 iv   Jona. Longfellow, b. 25 Jan , 1838, m 26 April, 1869, Mary P. Hubbard.

690 v   Greenleaf, b. 25 Aug., 1840, m. 25 June, 1874, Laura Williams.

* 691 vi   Sarah Lee, b. 29 Dec , 1843, m. 26 Jan , 1864, H. Benton Teetor.

692 vii   Caroline Louise, b. 31 Dec., 1846; died young.

211   Bradbury[7], m. Harriet, dau. of Elias and Elizabeth (——) Hedges. He was a person of great energy and industry, and acquired a large fortune.

"Bradbury had dark hair and eyes; was full six feet tall and well proportioned; was noted for his strength and that he needed no other protector nor protection than his own right arm—a blow from it would have been like a sledge hammer. He always lived at Colerain, near the old homestead. Was very successful in raising stock, and had excellent judgment in his real estate transactions. His estate was valued at about $400,000 " It will be noticed that many of his descendants bear the name of Bedinger. The ancestors of this family were pioneers in Kentucky, and the Bedingers are still living on the land once occupied by Daniel Boone.

693 i   Emily, b. 16 Feb., 1836, m. 3 June, 1857, James Poole, who b. 29 March, 1834. They lived in Groesbeck, Ham. Co., Ohio, and had : Ida, b. 1 May, 1858, Allyn Cilley, b. 18 Aug., 1860, Evelyn, b. 8 March, 1863, Ellen Hardin, b. 18 Jan., 1865, Harriet Hedges, b. 16 Dec., 1868, Bradbury Cilley, b. 26 Aug., 1873, and Emily, b. 26 June, 1876.

694 ii   Mary, b. 7 April, 1838, m. 25 Dec., 1860, Daniel Bedinger, b. 13 July, 1835. They reside in Richwood, Boone Co., Kentucky, and had: ' Harriet, b. 2 Dec., 1861, Daniel Everett, b. 24 March, 1863, Henry, b. 9 Feb., 1865, Jonathan Cilley, b. 22 Jan., 1867, Benjamin Franklin, b 18 June, 1869, Columbus Cilley, b. 24 March, 1871, Mary Cilley, b. 11 April, 1875, d. 24 June, 1877.

---

* Sarah and H. Benton Teetor had issue: Josephine Cilley, b. 27 Oct., 1867, Helen Dudley, b. 6 Dec., 1870, Howard Lee, b. 13 Sept., 1873.

† 695 iii Columbus, b. 4 Nov. 1839, m 30 Oct., 1867, Agnes Anderson, d. 28 Aug., 1872.

696 iv Elizabeth Ann, b. 12 July, 1842, m. 5 Feb., 1862, David Bedinger. They reside in Richwood, Boone Co , Kentucky, and had: Olivia Morgan, b. 30 Oct., 1862, Jessie, b. 29 Oct., 1864, Bradbury Cilley, b. 18 Aug., 1866, Ann Elizabeth, b. 27 Sept., 1868, Agnes, b. 22 March, 1871, Emily Daisey, b. 16 March, 1873.

697 v Harriet, b. 11 March, 1844, m. 1st, 19 May, 1863, Benj F. Bedinger, who was b 12 Oct., 1843, and d. 12 Sept. 1868, and had Benjamin F , b. 1 March, 1864, Henrietta Clay, b. 10 Aug., 1866, Harriet, b 16 Dec., 1868, m. 2d, 25 Nov., 1874, Alphonse C. Turner. They reside in Ross, Butler Co., Ohio, and have Edna, b 7 March, 1876.

698 vi Bradbury, b. 27 Nov , 1846, d. 19 Jun., 1850

699 vii Martha Ellen, b. 6 August, 1848, d. 22 Feb., 1849.

700 viii Sarah Jane Marsh, b. 17 March, 1853, m. 21 June. 1875, Silas Elder Moorhead, b. 5 June, 1853. They reside in Ham. Co., Ohio, and have Edith, b. 25 April, 1876.

217 Col. Joseph[7] was b. in Nottingham, N. H. Educated at Atkinson Academy. He was commissioned as Ensign in the 1st Co. of the 18th Regt, by Gov. Jno. Langdon, on the 17th Oct., 1811. On March 12th, 1812, he was appointed an Ensign in the U. S. Army, and ordered for duty in Capt. Jno. McClary's Co., 11th Regt, U. S. Infantry, then commanded by Col Isaac Clarke of Vt. He was promoted to Lieut. March 17th, 1814, transferred to the 21st U. S. Infantry commanded by Col. Miller, and was in the battle of Chippewa. In the battle of Bridgewater or "Lundy's Lane," he was badly wounded by a musket ball, producing a compound fracture of the thigh bone. Soon afterwards he was brevetted captain for his gallantry in that battle.

The action of the 21st Regiment in this engagement, deserves mention. The enemy, after his repulse at Chippewa, July 4, 1814, on the 25th of July appeared in force at Queenstown, and his fleet arrived and lay near Fort Niagara. Gen Scott, with the First Brigade, Towson artillery, and all the dragoons and cavalry, was ordered to march towards Queenstown, to report if the enemy appeared, and to call for assistance if necessary. Scott pushed on his command with vigor, and upon his arrival at the Falls found the enemy, under Gen. Riall, directly in front, behind a narrow strip of woods, and in line of battle upon Lundy's Lane—a ridge of land nearly at right angles with the Niagara, and about a mile below the falls. Gen. Scott sent information to Gen. Brown, and his advance commenced skirmishing about half-past 5 P. M.; but the action did not commence in earnest till near 7 P. M. The

British were in much larger force, and were able to extend their lines much further and to make flank movements. To counteract this advantage our troops fought in detachments and charged in column, each upon their own responsibility, until Gen. Brown came up with the remainder of the forces. Major Jessup taking advantage of a wood between a road parallel to the river and the river, through which he led his regiment, turned the enemy's left, took Gen. Riall and some of his principal officers prisoners, and charging back regained his position in gallant style. Meanwhile, the enemy moved a battalion to the rear of our right flank, but were promptly met by Major McNeil with the Eleventh, and driven back with great slaughter. Thus the contest raged for an hour; the British infantry driven back at each point by turns, but holding their position through a powerful battery of 2 twenty-fours, 4 sixes, and three howitzers, planted upon a rising ground and commanding the field, and keeping up a destructive and incessant fire.

Now came Ripley's brigade, containing Lieut. Cilley's regiment, to the front, greeted by cheer after cheer by the combatants, enveloped in smoke and mad with excitement. While forming for evening parade, the booming of cannon and rattle of small arms announced that Scott had found the enemy. They moved immediately, and at the double quick, actually running three miles betwixt the camp and the battle-field. Porter's brigade followed them. Both were soon deployed and hurled against the enemy, but the battery upon the hill made sad havoc among our troops. It became evident to Gen. Brown that the British battery must be carried, to insure success. He turned to gallant Miller of the 21st, and ordered him to storm the battery. " I'll try, sir," was the laconic reply. The contest that followed is well described in a letter written by Col. Miller:

" I had short of 300 men with me, as my regiment had been weakened by numerous details made from it during the day. I however immediately obeyed the order. We could see all their slow-matches and port-fires burning and ready. I did not know what side of the work had the most favorable approach, but happened to hit upon a very favorable place, notwithstanding we advanced upon the mouths of their pieces. There was an old rail fence on the side where we approached, undiscovered by the enemy, with a small growth of shrubbery by the fence, and within less than two rods of the cannons' mouth. I then very cautiously ordered my men to rest across the fence, take good aim, fire, and rush; which was done in style. Not a man at the cannons was left to put fire to them. We got into the center of their park before they had time to oppose us. A British line was formed and lying in strong position to protect their artillery; the moment we got to the center they opened a most destructive flank fire on us; killed a great many, and attempted to charge with their bayonets. We returned the fire so warmly they were compelled to stand. We fought hand to hand for some time, so close that the blaze of our guns crossed each other; but we compelled them to abandon their whole artillery, ammunition, wagons and all, amounting to seven pieces of elegant brass cannon, one of which was a twenty-four pounder, with eight horses and harnesses, though some of the horses were killed. The British made two more attempts to charge us at close quarters, both of which we repulsed before I was reinforced by the First and Twenty-third regiments; and even after that, the British charged with their whole line three several times, and after getting within half pistol shot of us were compelled to give way. I took with my regiment, between thirty and forty prisoners."

This charge took place about 10 o'clock at night, in moonlight. Col. Miller's regiment lost in killed, wounded and missing, one hundred and twenty-six, nearly one half its strength. Lieut. Cilley's company led in the charge on the guns, and every commissioned and every non-commissioned officer present with the company was either killed or wounded. This was one of the most sanguinary battles of the war, and the gallant act of Col. Miller and the noble Twenty-first was the admiration of every one.

He was in the battle of Chrystlers fields, on the St. Lawrence, and served through the war with distinction, and was retained in the army on the peace establishment, until he resigned his commission in July, 1816. An explosion of cartridges at Detroit, Mich., caused the loss of his right eye. On the 21st June, 1817, he was commissioned as Quartermaster on the staff of the 1st Div. N. H. Militia, and in 1821 as Div. Inspector, and in 1827 appointed an aide upon the staff of Gov. Benjamin Pierce. In 1846 he was elected by the Legislature to the U. S. Senate, to fill the vacancy caused by the resignation of Hon. Levi Woodbury. Upon the close of his senatorial term, Col. Cilley returned to his farm in Nottingham. There he remains in the quiet enjoyment of a competence, with the reputation of a brave and gallant soldier, an upright and honorable man, and has the respect and esteem of his fellow men. Although in his 88th year, his faculties, excepting his eyesight, are remarkably good, and his judgment is as sound and as much sought after as ever.

He m. 15 Dec., 1824, Elizabeth, dau. of Nathaniel and Anna (Cilley 68) Williams, who d. Jan. 25, 1843.

701 i   Nathaniel Williams, b. 10 Sept., 1825, unmarried, d. 4 Oct., 1855.

702 ii   * Martha Ann, b. 2 April, 1827, m. 4 May, 1853, Dr. Chas. S. Downes and had: i Bessie Williams, b. 7 March, 1855, d. 21 March, 1869. ii Frederick Cilley, b. 26 Oct., 1864, d. 15 Feb., 1869. iii Joseph Cilley, b. 15 April, 1870.

703 iii   Enoch Poor, b 4 June, 1829, ⎱ Twins, unmarried, d. 11 July, 1873.
704 iv   Greenleaf Longfellow, b. 4 June, 1829, ⎰ d. 11 June, 1836.

705 v   Victoria Elizabeth, b 24 Sept., 1831, m. 29 April, 1857, Thomas Bradbury Bartlett, and had: i Nathaniel Cilley, b 22 June, 1858. A student at Harvard College. ii Anne Elizabeth, b. 18 Feb., 1861. iii Joseph Bradbury, b. 11 Feb., 1863. iv Mary Victoria, b. 22 April, 1865. v Jennie Nealley, b. 2 March, 1871. vi Benjamin Thomas, b. 9 Nov. 1872.

† 706 vi   Joseph Nealley, b. 15 Feb., 1833, m. 19 Aug., 1874, Mary Butler.

707 vii   Jennie Osborne, b. 28 Oct , 1836, unmarried, d. 11 Sept , 1876.

708 viii   Jonathan, b. 19 July 1838, d. 15 Jan , 1858.

709 ix   Frederick, b. 21 Feb., 1841, d. 17 April, 1861.

221 Hon. Jonathan[7], b. 2 July, 1802, in Nottingham, N. H., Prepared for College at Atkinson Academy, N. H. Entered Bowdoin College, and graduated in the celebrated class of 1825. Moved to Thomaston, Me., and commenced the practice of law; m. Deborah, b. 6 July, 1808, d. 14 Aug., 1844, dau. of Hon. Hezekiah and Isabella (Coombs) Prince. (Vide the Prince Genealogy in note.) Was elected member of the Legislature in 1831–33–34–35. In 1835–6 was elected Speaker of the House, and in 1836 was elected Representative to the 25th Congress. Was killed in a duel with the Hon. W. J. Graves, M. C. of Kentucky, Feb. 24, 1838, near Washington, D. C.

Hawthorne in his American notes, thus speaks of him under date of Friday, July 28, 1837 : "Saw my classmate and intimate friend Cilley for the first time since we graduated. He has met with good success in life, in spite of circumstances, having struggled upward against bitter opposition, by the force of his own abilities, to be a member of Congress after having been for some time the leader of his own party in the State Legislature. We met like old friends, and conversed almost as freely as we

used to in college days, twelve years ago and more. He is a
singular person, shrewd, crafty, insinuating, with wonderful tact,
seizing on each man by his manageable point, and using him for
his own purpose. His conversation was full of natural feeling,
the expression of which can hardly be misunderstood, and his
revelations with regard to himself had really a great deal of frankness. He spoke of his ambition, of the obstacles he had encoun-
tered, of the means by which he had overcome them, imputing
great efficacy to his personal intercourse with people, and his
study of their characters ; then of his course as a member of the
legislature and Speaker, and his style of speaking and its effects.
Then as to his private affairs, he spoke of his marriage, of his
wife, his children, and told me, with tears in his eyes, of the death
of a dear little girl, and how it effected him, and how impossible
it had been for him to believe that she was really to die. A man
of the most open nature might well have been more reserved to a
friend, after twelve years of separation, than Cilley was to me.
He by no means feigns the good feeling that he professes, nor is
there anything affected in the frankness of his conversation, and it
is that which makes him so very fascinating. There is such a
quantity of truth and kindliness and warm affections, that a man's
heart opens to him, in spite of himself. He deceives by truth,
and is, when occasion demands, bold and fierce as a tiger ; deter-
mined, and even straightforward and undisguised in his measures."

The news of his death produced intense excitement in Thomaston. Friend and foe joined alike in the general mourning and in
the warmest tributes to his worth. A large meeting was held
March 7, 1838, at which strong resolutions, reported by a com-
mittee of 43, were adopted ; expressions of the intense feeling of
sorrow and indignation that pervaded the community. An ode,
composed for the occasion, by Mrs. Woodhull, was sung, and
speeches made by L. H. Chandler, Herman Stevens, J. O'Brien,
J. S. Abbot, P. Keegan, Beder Fales, S. C. Fessenden and W. J.
Farley. The latter said : " We were always political opponents
and professional rivals, but amid all the bitterness of party strife,
in all the warmth of professional controversy, our personal friend-
ship was never for a moment interrupted. Mr. Cilley was politi-
cally a warm partizan. Of an ardent temperament, burning for
distinction, conscious of powers with which God had endowed
him, and fearless in the expression of his feelings, it was impos-

sible that he should not make enemies as well as friends." Never was a duel pressed to a fatal close in the face of such open kindness as was expressed by Mr. Cilley. His error was a generous one, since he fought for what he deemed the honor of New England. He said to a friend just before the fatal day, "I am driven to this meeting by a positive compulsion. I have done all that an honorable man can do to avert it. Why should I acknowledge that man (Webb) to be a gentlemen and a man of honor? In truth and conscience I could not do so, and still less can I have it so unreasonably extorted from me by force and threat. I have no ill-will nor disrespect towards Graves. He knows it, and I have repeatedly and fully expressed it. I abhor the idea of taking his life, and will do nothing not forced upon me in self-defense. The pretext of the challenge is absurd. I understand the conspiracy to destroy me as a public man. *But New England must not be trampled on*! and I go to this field sustained by as high a motive of patriotism as ever led my grandfather or brother to battle; as an unhappy duty, not to be shrunk from, to my honor, my principles, and my country." He died a martyr to the right of free speech.

† 710 i   Greenleaf, b. 27 Oct., 1829, m 13 May, 1860, Malvina Vernet.

  711 ii   Jane Nealley, b. 31 July, 1831, d. 19 May, 1836.

  712 iii   Bowdoin Longfellow, b. 1 Sept, 1833, d. 25 June, 1834.

† 713 iv   Jonathan Prince, b. 29 Dec., 1835, m. 10 Oct., 1866, Caroline A. Lazell, who d. 7 April, 1871.

  714 v   Julia Draper, b. 20 Dec., 1837; m. 27 Jan., 1864, Ellis D., son of the Rev. Jonathan Ellis and Julia Ann (Draper) Lazell of Spencer, Mass. He was b. 7 May, 1832, and d. in Rockland, Me., 13 Feb., 1875. He served during the war of the Rebellion as Lieut. and Quartermaster in the Garabaldi Guards, 39th N. Y. Vols. Was Captain and A. Q. M. on the staff of Stahl's Brigade. They had: i James Draper, b 16 April 1867. ii Ellis Warren, b. 11 Oct., 1869. iii Theodore Studley, b. 20 Aug., 1871.

NOTE OF THE PRINCE GENEALOGY.

John Prince, Rector of East Shefford in Berkshire, Eng., m. Elizabeth, dau. of the Rev Dr. Tolderburg, and had: i John, b. in E. Shefford, 1610, m. 1st, Alice Honour, 2d, Anne, d. 16 Aug, 1676; ii Francis, a merchant in London; iii and iv sons; v, vi, vii, viii, ix, x, xi, daughters.

John (2) b. 1610, in E. Shefford; was at Watertown, N. E., about 1633, then at Hingham: settled at Nantasket, 1638: 1st Ruling Elder at Hull, 1644, and d. there. Issue by 1st wife only—i John, b. 1638: ii Elizabeth, b. 1640, m. about 1662, Josiah Loring, who d. 17 Feb., 1713-14: she d. 13 May, 1727. †iii Joseph, b. 1643⅗, m. 7 Dec., 1670, Joanna Morton: d. 1695. iv Martha, b. 1645, m. Chs. Wheaton. †v Job, b. 1647, m. Rebecca —: d. 1694. †vi Samuel, b. May, 1649, m. 1st, 9 Dec., 1674, Martha Barstow: 2d, Mercy Hinkley, d. 3 July, 1723. vii Benjamin, b. 1652, d. at Jamaica, W. I. †viii Isaac, b. 1654, m. 24 Dec., 1679, Mary Turner, d. 7 Nov., 1718. †ix Thomas, b. 1658, m. Ruth Turner, d. 1704.

Thomas (3), bap. 3 Aug , at Scituate, Mass., m. Ruth, dau. of John Turner, Sen., of Scituate, d. at Barbadoes, 1704: had i Thomas, b. 1686: ii James, b. 1687: iii Ruth, b. 1689: iv Benjamin, b. 1693, m. 1 April, 1717, Abiel Nelson: †v Job, b. 1695, m. Abagail Kimball.

Job (4), m. Abagail Kimball, and had: i Thomas, b. ——: ii Job, b.——; †iii Kimball, b. 9 May, 1726, m. 13 Nov., 1749, Deborah Fuller; iv James, b.——; v Christopher, b.——: vi Ruth, b.——.

Kimball, m. Deborah, dau. of Deacon John Fuller, and had: i Christopher, b. 22 July, 1751: ii Kimball, 2d, b. 29 July, 1753: iii Sarah, b. 15 Jan., 1756: iv Ruth, b. 7 May, 1758: v Deborah, b. 13 July, 1760: vi Noah, b. 18 Jan., 1763: vii Job, b. 22 May, 1765: viii John, b. 23 Feb., 1768.

ix Hezekiah (6), b. 7 Feb., 1771, m 4 Jan., 1798, Isabella, dau. of Lt. Joseph and Elizabeth (Gamble) Coombs, who was b. 9 April, 1781, and d. 2 Dec , 1840. He d. 27 Dec., 1840. They had: i Eliza, b. 14 Oct., 1798, m. 1817, Wm. Pope of Spencer, Mass., d. 25 July, 1828: ii Hezekiah, 2d, b. 8 Oct., 1800, m. 23 Oct., 1828, Henrietta Marsh, d. 26 July, 1843: iii Sarah, b. 20 July, 1802, m. Jan., 1823, Dr. David Kellogg: iv Isabella, b. 10 Feb., 1805, m. 24 June, 1827, Jno. B. H. Starr, living in Spencer, Mass.: v Deborah, b. 6 July, 1808, m. 2 April, 1829, Hon. Jonathan Cilley, d. 14 Aug., 1844; vi Lucy, b. 25 Aug., 1810, m. 5 July, 1836, E. S. J. Nealley, Esq., d. 17 Sept., 1853; vii Joseph, b. 16 Sept., 1814, m. 12 Sept., 1837, Lucinda A. Walker, d. 10 Sept., 1843; viii George, b. 9 Aug., 1817, m. 29 April, 1845, Lucy M. Rice, living in Bath, Me.; ix Nancy Pope. b. 25 May, 1820, m. 19 Oct., 1842, Rev. Lorenzo B. Allen, d 1858: x Christopher, b. 31 July, 1822, m. 3 May, 1846, Marion W. Webb, living in Thomaston, Me.

225 Samuel Plumer[7], b. in Nottingham; m. Hannah H. Critchett, b. in Epsom, 6 Oct., 1801, and d. there 21 June, 1875.

715 i Joseph, b. 25 March, 1831. Unmarried. He was one of the first to enlist in the late war of the rebellion. Served 3 mos. in the 1st R. I. Cavalry, and was honorably discharged. Re-enlisted 20th Jan., 1862, and remained in active service in Virginia until Feb., 1865, when he returned to Concord, N. H., as a recruiting officer, and while thus employed died in Chichester, N. H., 6 March, 1865.

†716 ii Daniel Thomas, b. 1 May, 1834, m. 4 July, 1859, Lydia A. Babb.

717 iii Hannah P., b. 16 April, 1837, m. 1st, 8 May, 1858, Elbridge L. Swain of Northwood, who served in the 11th N. H., and d. at Newport News, Va., 17 March, 1863: 2d, 10 Oct., 1871, Chas. A. Steele of Chichester.

228 Rev. Daniel Plumer[7], m. Adelaide Ayres, b. 13 Jan., 1813, dau. of Abner and Elizabeth P. (Ayres) Haines of Canterbury, N. H. Was ordained 6 Feb., 1833, as pastor, and served as such in Northwood and New Market, until 1839, when he removed to Pittsfield and remained there four years. In 1843 he was called to his pastorate in Manchester, N. H., and remained there seven years. Declining health caused his resignation, and after two years in the country he regained his health and moved to Boston and lived there five years. Served two years at Great Falls, N. H., and three years in Farmington. Here he was given leave of absence by the church to enter the 8th N. H. Vols., as Chaplain, com. 4 Nov., 1861. Served in the Dept. of the Gulf, under Gens. B. F. Butler and N. P. Banks, and was in every action in which his regiment took part. It suffered severely at Port Hudson and in the Red river campaign. When his regiment was disbanded at the expiration of its enlistment, he was commissioned as Chaplain of the 2nd New York Veteran Cavalry, and was with his regiment until honorably mustered out in December, 1865, when the civil war was virtually closed. He was sent as a missionary by the American Missionary Association to Alabama, but soon compelled to return North by ill-health. He resides at present in Farmington, N. H.

During the Rev. Daniel's active years he married between 700 and 800 couples, baptised about 1000 people, and attended many funerals. He has the pleasant consciousness of knowing that he invariably left his churches in a very much more prosperous condition than he found them.

†718 i Clinton Albert, b. 16 Feb., 1837, m. 9 Sept., 1868, Emma S. Harper of N. C.

 719 ii Adelaide Haines, b. 23 Feb., 1843, in Manchester, N. H., m. 1st, 1 May, 1862, Dr. Nathan, son of Dr. D. T and Clara C Parker: he d. 31 Dec., 1866. 2d, 15 Aug., 1871, John Waldron, Esq., of Farmington. Issue: 1 Adelaide Cecil, b. 17 May, 1872. ii Elizabeth Pearl, b. 25 Aug., 1873.

 720 iii Emma Stark, b. 21 Sept., 1851: d. 19 Sept., 1852.

 721 iv Daniel Plummer, Jr., b. 27 Nov., 1854, m. 19 May, 1875, Velma A. Waldron.

 722 v Joseph Bradbury, b. 25 April, 1856, in Boston.

230 William Plumer,[7] m. 1st, Emmeline, dau. of Samuel and Abigail (Goss) Whitney, b. June 8, 1806, d. 27 Oct., 1861; 2d, Nancy J. Dudley nee Ames, dau. of Parker Ames.

† 723 i Charles Whitney, b. 5 Aug., 1836, m. 25 May, 1858, Ann M. Ames.

 724 ii Abbie Whitney, b 24 July, 1839, m. 25 Nov., 1858, Clifton B. Hildreth of Suncook, N. H.

 725 iii George H., b. 24 July, 1843, d. 2 April, 1863.

By 2d wife:

726 iv Emma, b. 11 April, 1864.

231 Jonathan Longfellow[7], twin brother to Wm. P., m. Harriet, dau. of Samuel and Abigail (Goss) Whitney.

727 i Helen Maria, b. Jan., 1833, unmarried, d. 185—.

728 ii Antoinette, b. ——, m. Thomas Jones.

729 iii Harriet Jane, b. ——, 184—, m. Col. John George.

233 Joseph Longfellow[7], married Lavinia Bagley, dau. of the Hon. John Kelley of Exeter. Resided in Nottingham and Exeter.

† 730 i   Bradbury Longfellow, b. Sept. 6, 1838, m. July 3, 1864, Amanda C. Morris.
† 731 ii   John Kelly, b. 13 April, 1840, m. 14 April, 1868, Helen L. Hutchins.
† 732 iii   Jacob Poor, b. 10 June, 1841, m. 22 Sept., 1870, Eugenia E. Davis.
   733 iv   Joseph Longfellow, b. 23 Dec , 1842. Graduated at Harvard in 1864. During the rebellion served as a Civil Clerk in the Quartermaster's Department for one year.
   734 v   Charles Emery, b. 20 March, 1845, d. 2 May, 1845.
   735 vi   Alice Lavina, b. 6 Dec., 1848.
   736 vii   George Enoch, b. 29 April, 1851.
   737 viii   Edward Hilton, b. 2 July, 1855.
   738 ix   Harriet Susan, b. 25 March, 1856.
   739 x   Emma, b. 2 Jan., 1860.

234 John Osgood resides in Nottingham and Pittsfield. A farmer ; m. Henrietta Butler, b. Dec. 24, 1813, dau. of Ebenezer and Sally (Hersey) Butler of Nottingham.

   740 i   Laura Osgood, b. 5 March, 1834, m. 27 Nov., 1856, Wm. Henry Berry of Pittsfield.*
   741 ii   Walter Longfellow, b. 24 Feb., 1836. Died at Manchester, 21 Feb., 1857.
   742 iii   Harriet Poor, b. 3 May, 1838, m. 29 Aug., 1860, Wm. B. Blake of Raymond, d. 11 July, 1873; had Mable C , b. 20 July, 1862.
   743 iv   Martha Butler, b. 29 Jan., 1841, d. 23 June, 1849.
   744 v   Sarah Hersey, b. 19 Nov., 1843, m. 16 June, 1869, Jas. D. Butler.†
   745 vi   Henrietta Butler, b. 3 Aug., 1845, m. 3 Aug., 1865, Benj. Dow Mathews of Lee.; have Albert, b. 11 Apr., 1867, Florence, b. 26 June, 1869.
   746 vii   John Henry, b. 24 Feb., 1848.
   747 viii   Frank Osgood, b. 16 Aug., 1851, d. 18 Jan., 1853.

236 Jacob Green, m. 1st, 1845, Emma Stark, a descendant of Gen. Stark of Revolutionary fame, who died without issue, 16 Feb., 1859; 2nd, 29 Jan., 1861, Martha Cilley, dau. of Rev. Nathaniel and Elizabeth Ann (Cilley) Bouton. A manufacturer in Manchester, N. H.

   748 i   Harry, b. 13 May, 1862.
   749 ii   Florence, b. ——. Died young.

238 Bradbury Poor.[7] Graduated at Dartmouth, 1843; lawyer, Manchester. Was elected Mayor of Manchester in 1877, (Aug.) but declined the office. Was Colonel on Gov. Goodwin's staff, 1859 and 1861.

   750 i   Martha Poor, b. 20 Feb., 1859.

---

*CHILDREN—Walter Cilley, b. Dec. 6, 1862, William, b. July 13, 1866, Grace, b. Dec. 6, 1872.

† ISSUE—Paul, b. Oct. 18, 1870, Mary, b. July 9, 1874.

240 Horatio Gates[7], graduated at Dartmouth College in 1827, read law with G. Sullivan at Exeter. Practised in South Deerfield, N. H., and Lewiston, Maine.

† 751 i Horatio Gates, b. 1 Nov., 1841, m. 16 Jan , 1868, Julia A. Harrington.
  752 ii John Jenness, b. 31 Aug., 1843. Resides in E. Boston, Mass.

247 Joseph Bradbury.[7] A farmer.

753 i Bradbury J., b. 30 July, 1860. A student at Phillips Academy, Exeter.

250 Joseph[7], (commonly called Joe Jackson) was published 23 Feb., 1822, to Nancy Maloon of Deerfield, N. H. Was a farmer.

  754 i   Louisa, b. 12 Nov., 1823, m. Sam'l R. Thompson, Barrington, N. H.
  755 ii Julia A , b. 1826, m. Abram Cilley of Northwood.
† 756 iii George B., b. 2 Dec., 1828, m. 9 May, 1855, Lydia Smith, d. 11 Feb., 1874.
  757 iv Irene, b. Dec., 1831: d. 4 Jan., 1853.
  758 v   Harriet, b. July, 1835, m. Alex. Marden, E. Haverhill, N. H.
† 759 vi David, b. 18 Aug., 1837, m. 31 Aug., 1863, Sylvina L. Tuttle.
  760 vii Jacob, b. 11 May, 1840, m. Mary Bodwell: lives in Providence, R.I. No issue.
  761 viii Josephine, b. Aug., 1842, m. 1st, —— Bryant of New Market: 2d, —— True.
  762 ix Emma, b 22 Aug., 1846, m. Jno. P. Watson, Pittsfield, N. H.

www.ingramcontent.com/pod-product-compliance
Lightning Source LLC
Chambersburg PA
CBHW060656280326
41933CB00012B/2206